International labour standards

AF791053

International labour standards

A workers' education manual   Fourth (revised) edition

International Labour Office   Geneva

Copyright © International Labour Organization 1998
First published 1978
Fourth edition 1998

Publications of the International Labour Office enjoy copyright under Protocol 2 of the Universal Copyright Convention. Nevertheless, short excerpts from them may be reproduced without authorization, on condition that the source is indicated. For rights of reproduction or translation, application should be made to the Publications Bureau (Rights and Permissions), International Labour Office, CH-1211 Geneva 22, Switzerland. The International Labour Office welcomes such applications.

Libraries, institutions and other users registered in the United Kingdom with the Copyright Licensing Agency, 90 Tottenham Court Road, London W1P 9HE (Fax: +44 171 436 3986), in the United States with the Copyright Clearance Center, 222 Rosewood Drive, Danvers, MA 01923 (Fax: +1 508 750 4470), or in other countries with associated Reproduction Rights Organizations, may make photocopies in accordance with the licences issued to them for this purpose.

ILO
International labour standards. A workers' education manual (fourth edition)
Geneva, International Labour Office, 1998

/Workers' education course/, /ILO Convention/, /ILO Recommendation/.01.03.7
ISBN 92-2-110330-7

Also published in Spanish: *Las normas internacionales del trabajo* (ISBN 92-2-310330-4), Geneva, 1998

Also published in French: *Les normes internationales du travail* (ISBN 92-2-210330-0), Geneva, 1998

ILO Cataloguing in Publication Data

The designations employed in ILO publications, which are in conformity with United Nations practice, and the presentation of material therein do not imply the expression of any opinion whatsoever on the part of the International Labour Office concerning the legal status of any country, area or territory or of its authorities, or concerning the delimitation of its frontiers.

The responsibility for opinions expressed in signed articles, studies and other contributions rests solely with their authors, and publication does not constitute an endorsement by the International Labour Office of the opinions expressed in them.

Reference to names of firms and commercial products and processes does not imply their endorsement by the International Labour Office, and any failure to mention a particular firm, commercial product or process is not a sign of disapproval.

ILO publications can be obtained through major booksellers or ILO local offices in many countries, or direct from ILO Publications, International Labour Office, CH-1211 Geneva 22, Switzerland. Catalogues or lists of new publications are available free of charge from the above address.

Photocomposed in Switzerland/Printed in France WEI/JOU

Contents

Introduction

This is one in a series of ILO workers' education manuals dealing with matters of concern to or forming part of the functions of the International Labour Organisation. Its first edition was made possible thanks to generous contributions received from the Governments of Norway and Sweden.

Whereas other manuals in the series deal with subjects such as freedom of association, collective bargaining, wages, economics, labour inspection and workers' education, the present one is concerned with the standard-setting work of the ILO. It traces the origins and the development of this action up to the present day; describes the procedures for the adoption of international labour standards in the form of Conventions and Recommendations; provides a bird's-eye view of the vast body of international labour standards so far adopted; analyses the procedures – supervisory or promotional – developed over the years to ensure effective and widespread application of those standards; outlines the special complaints procedures that exist to deal with alleged violations of ILO Conventions; and reviews the special procedures that exist as regards freedom of association and trade union rights. A final chapter is devoted to the practical effect that Conventions and Recommendations have had over the years among the many member States of the ILO.

This manual is intended to provide guidance for workers' education instructors and trade union officials, that is, for people who conduct workers' education courses or study groups. It should also be of special interest to trade unionists who play a particularly direct part in the standard-setting activities of the ILO or who may wish to know more about international labour standards from the point of view of their value in day-to-day union work.

In addition, it is hoped that the manual will also be read by people outside the trade union movement. Law students, industrial relations experts, legislators and ordinary citizens interested in human rights, labour and social matters are likely to find this book useful for their purposes.

Throughout the manual, actual examples have been given of the practical application of the procedures described. This has necessitated reference to cases involving specific countries. It should, however, be stressed that these examples serve as illustrations only, and are not intended to highlight or comment upon the current situation in any particular country. A classified guide to international labour standards and a select bibliography will be found at the back of the manual.

Chapter 1

The ILO as a standard-setting organisation

Origins and history

The principal originator of the idea of international labour legislation, and precursor of the work of the International Labour Organisation, was Daniel Le Grand (1783-1859), a French manufacturer who from 1840 to 1853 repeatedly appealed to several European governments for joint agreement on labour legislation as a means of eliminating merciless competition. He also worked on several projects for establishing international labour laws covering hours of work, a day of rest, night work, unhealthy or dangerous occupations and special rules for children. These projects were very carefully drafted after a study of the legal position in different countries – in much the same way as the International Labour Office prepares draft standards today.

Daniel Le Grand (1783-1859) was a pioneer in the field of international labour legislation. His proposed labour laws on working life and conditions could be seen as forerunners of the international labour Conventions developed by the ILO.

The first international conferences

Le Grand died without seeing his projects brought to fruition, but the idea found other advocates, first through private initiatives such as the International Benevolent Congresses which met in 1856 and 1857 and adopted a motion in favour of the drafting in common of international measures for the regulation of industrial labour as a means of promoting and extending the action taken by leading industrialists for the protection of the workers, and later in the fast-growing trade union movement, which was beginning to forge international links of its own.

Meanwhile, domestic laws to restrict child labour and in some cases women's work had been adopted in a number of countries. Forward-looking politicians were beginning to feel that these and similar measures should be standardised and extended by international agreement, and the possibilities were discussed particularly in the French and German Parliaments. The first positive initiative came from Switzerland when in 1889 the Federal Council sent out invitations to 13 governments to attend a preliminary conference to consider the points of labour law which it would be desirable to regulate by international convention. The opening of the conference was fixed for 5 May 1890 in Berne, but, in view of action taken in Germany to convene a similar gathering, the Swiss Federal Council decided to abandon its own conference and give its support to the German project. The result was an international factory and mine labour conference, better known as the Berlin conference, which opened on 15 March 1890. It sat for two weeks, producing detailed recommendations for the regulation or prohibition of child labour, and regulation of mine labour, Sunday work, child labour, employment of young persons and women, but no international commitments were formally entered into.

The Berlin conference appears to have had little direct effect, but it is historic in that it was the first occasion when governments came together to discuss labour standards, and the conference undoubtedly paved the way for future action.

The first International Labour Office

Seven years after the Berlin conference, in August 1897, nearly 400 delegates, representing Christian workers' organisations from 14 countries, met in Zurich for a conference entitled the "First International Congress on Labour Protection". This congress passed a resolution requesting the Swiss Government to resume its efforts to promote international labour legislation and in particular to "issue an invitation to the various governments to set up a labour office".

Another conference was held in Brussels in September 1897 to examine the achievements of the Berlin conference and to study the principles on which an international labour office should be established. The conference was composed of eminent scholars and parliamentarians from Europe and America. It was the brainchild of Professor Ernest

Mahaim from Belgium, who was later to become Chairman of the ILO Governing Body.

As a direct outcome of the conference, a committee was appointed to promote the idea in various countries. Several national organisations devoted to the concept were formed. They first met at a conference in Paris in July 1900 which founded the International Association for Labour Legislation, the immediate forerunner of the ILO. The Swiss Canton of Basle presented the Association with suitable headquarters, and the first International Labour Office was opened on May Day 1901.

The First ***International Labour Office*** was established by the International Association for Labour Legislation, and opened on 1 May 1901, in Basle, Switzerland.

The International Association for Labour Legislation was not an organisation of governments: its members were the various national associations which had been campaigning for international action, but governments willing to accept its objectives could be represented on the international committee, which met every two years. The Governments of France, Italy, the Netherlands and Switzerland were represented from the outset, and by the time the First World War brought its activities to a standstill 22 governments were associated with the organisation.

The Association held two international conferences, in Berne in 1905 and 1906, at which 13 States were represented – Denmark, France, Germany, Greece, Italy, Luxembourg, the Netherlands, Portugal, Romania, Serbia, Spain, Switzerland and the United Kingdom. The 1906 conference adopted two international treaties, one prohibiting the use of white phosphorus and the other regulating night work by women. These were the first international labour Conventions.

The white phosphorus Convention was ratified by all the signatories, plus Norway, which had not been able to attend the Berne conferences. The Convention concerning the night work of women was ratified by all but two, one of which, however, enacted similar legislation without formally ratifying the treaty.

In September 1913 the International Association called a third Berne conference in which 13 States participated. Two Conventions, one regulating working hours of women and children and the second prohibiting night work of children, were drafted. However, the First World War broke out before the relevant international treaties were concluded, and the war brought the effective history of the International Association for Labour Legislation to a close.

The founding of the ILO

As early as November 1914, the American Federation of Labor, at a congress held in Philadelphia, adopted a resolution calling for -

> a meeting of representatives of organised labor of the different nations to meet at the same time and place ... [as the general peace congress to be held at the close of the war] ... to the end that suggestions may be made and such action taken as shall be helpful in restoring fraternal relations, protecting the interests of the toilers, and thereby assisting in laying foundations for a more lasting peace.

Two years later, in 1916, a trade union conference was held in Leeds, United Kingdom, under the joint auspices of the British and French labour movements. Delegations from Belgium and Italy also took part. Among the personalities prominent at the conference was Léon Jouhaux, later to be leader of the workers' representatives in the ILO for many years, and Nobel Peace Prize winner in 1951. The Leeds conference moved that certain guarantees for workers, covering broadly hours of work, social security and occupational safety, should be included in the peace treaty. It also called for the establishment of an international commission to supervise the application of those provisions and to arrange future international conferences at which the range of international labour standards could be extended. A significant point was that the commission should include workers' and employers' representatives. Thirdly, the Leeds conference called for the creation of a permanent international labour office. Here was the germ of the ILO as we know it today.

The entry of the United States into the war in 1917 meant that the American Federation of Labor could be expected to add its weight to these proposals, which in effect complemented its own earlier resolution. In the same year, 1917, labour delegates from the Central European and neutral States met in Berne to formulate demands that were not fundamentally different from those of the Leeds conference. Thus, while the war was still raging, workers' organisations on all sides were moving towards the same goals.

As the war drew to an end, further meetings were held at which these organisations further elaborated their proposals. Two conferences were held in London, in February and September 1918, which brought together representatives of the workers of the Allied Powers on the initiative of the Labour Party and the Trades Union Congress of Great Britain. They demanded that labour should be represented at the peace conference, and that a world conference of labour and socialism should be held simultaneously. On the initiative of the American Federation of Labor, the September conference also adopted a series of principles which, it was hoped, would be included in the peace treaty itself, as an international labour charter that would constitute the foundation of social justice throughout the world. Several of those principles were eventually incorporated in the provisions constituting the International Labour Organisation.

When the peace conference met in 1919, it went further, in one respect, than the trade unions had demanded: one of its first acts was to appoint a Commission on International Labour Legislation to draw up proposals for inclusion in the treaty. The Commission was *tripartite*, i.e. with representatives from governments, the trade unions and the employers. It met for two months under the chairmanship of the American trade union leader, Samuel Gompers. The text it drafted became Part XIII of the Treaty of Versailles, which thus created the International Labour Organisation. Most of its provisions are still in effect and remain the Constitution of the Organization. The Preamble to the ILO Constitution declares that "universal and lasting peace can be established only if it is based upon social justice".

Among the various texts that the Commission prepared was a "Labour Charter" of nine principles to guide the policy of member States and of the ILO, which were embodied in the peace treaty:

— labour should not be regarded merely as a commodity or an article of commerce;

— the right of association;

— the payment of an adequate wage to maintain a reasonable standard of living;

— an eight-hour day or a 48-hour week;

— a weekly rest of at least 24 hours;

— the abolition of child labour;

— equal pay for equal work;

— equitable economic treatment of all workers in a country (i.e. immigrants as well as nationals);

— an inspection system to ensure the enforcement of the laws for workers' protection.

These principles were later widened, as we shall see, in the "Declaration of Philadelphia".

The Paris Peace Conference established the ***Commission on International Labour Legislation*** to draw up proposals for inclusion in the peace treaty. It drew up a Labour Charter to guide the policy of future member States of the ILO. The Commission recommended the creation of the International Labour Organisation, and this was brought into effect by the Treaty of Versailles.

Subsequent growth

The First Session of the International Labour Conference, which is the supreme body of the ILO, was held in Washington in October 1919. The man chosen to become the first Director of the new International Labour Office (which is the secretariat of the International Labour Organisation) was Albert Thomas of France. A former journalist, politician, and wartime Cabinet Minister, Thomas guided the ILO during its formative years.

Between the two world wars the ILO was an autonomous part of the League of Nations. The most urgent problems of the time, on which its first decisions were made, included the promotion of the eight-hour working day, the struggle against unemployment, social security, maternity protection and the working conditions of women and youth.

During the Second World War the ILO moved its headquarters to Montreal, Canada. In Philadelphia, in 1944, the International Labour Conference helped to prepare the ILO for the problems awaiting it after the war, and further defined the Organisation's aims and objectives in adopting the so-called "Declaration of Philadelphia", which is now an annex to the Constitution.

This text first reaffirms the fundamental principles on which the ILO is based, in particular that:

> (a) labour is not a commodity;
>
> (b) freedom of expression and of association are essential to sustained progress;
>
> (c) poverty anywhere constitutes a danger to prosperity everywhere;
>
> (d) the war against want requires to be carried on with unrelenting vigour within each nation, and by continuous and concerted international effort in which the representatives of workers and employers, enjoying equal status with those of governments, join with them in free discussion and democratic decision with a view to the promotion of the common welfare.

Next, the Declaration affirms what should be the central aim and criteria of national and international policies and measures:

> all human beings, irrespective of race, creed or sex, have the right to pursue both their material well-being and their spiritual development in conditions of freedom and dignity, of economic security and equal opportunity.

The ILO has –

"the solemn obligation to further among the nations of the world programmes which will achieve:

— full employment and the raising of standards of living;
— the employment of workers in the occupations in which they can have the satisfaction of giving the full measure of their skill and attainments and make their greatest contribution to the common well-being;
— the provision, with adequate guarantees for all concerned, of facilities for training and the transfer of labour, including migration for employment and settlement;
— policies in regard to wages and earnings, hours and other conditions of work calculated to ensure a just share of the fruits of progress to all, and a minimum living wage to all employed and in need of such protection;
— the effective recognition of the right of collective bargaining, the cooperation of management and labour in the continuous improvement of productive efficiency, and the collaboration of workers and employers in the preparation and application of social and economic measures;
— the extension of social security measures to provide a basic income to all in need of such protection and comprehensive medical care;
— adequate protection for the life and health of workers in all occupations;
— provision for child welfare and maternity protection; the provision of adequate nutrition, housing and facilities for recreation and culture;
— the assurance of equality of educational and vocational opportunity."

In 1946 the ILO became the first ***specialised agency*** of the United Nations, recognised as having special responsibility for social and labour questions.

In the social field the ILO has played an active part in one of the most striking changes since the Second World War, namely the large-scale development of international technical co-operation. ILO efforts are directed essentially towards the protection of basic human rights, the improvement of living and working conditions and the promotion of full employment. However, new problems continue to arise as a result of technological, economic and social change, and as a result the ILO now also has to deal with matters such as new technology, multinational corporations, globalisation and the working environment.

The ILO remains a standard-setting body, but today there is also a marked emphasis on operational programmes and on educational work. This has resulted, in particular, in the establishment of the International Institute for Labour Studies in Geneva in 1960, and of the International Training Centre of the ILO in Turin in 1965. The Institute specialises in higher education and research in the fields of social and labour policy, whereas the Turin Centre provides key personnel with training at a higher level than they can obtain in their home countries in areas such as vocational training, management development and training for trade unionists.

The expansion of ILO operational programmes, particularly the World Employment Programme, has been largely responsible for accelerating the effort to decentralise responsibilities from Geneva headquarters to the various regions of the world. In fact, expenditure on technical co-operation today represents about half of the total resources at the disposal of the ILO. The ILO had 174 member States in 1998, as compared with 45 at its foundation in 1919 and 58 immediately after the Second World War.

Structure

The International Labour Organisation is composed of a general assembly, the International Labour Conference, which meets every year; an executive council, the Governing Body; and a permanent secretariat, the International Labour Office. The Organisation also works through other bodies such as regional conferences, industrial committees and panels of experts.

The Conference

The International Labour Conference elects the Governing Body; adopts the ILO's budget, financed by contributions from member States; sets international labour standards and supervises their application (according to procedures which will be described later); passes resolutions which provide guide-lines for the ILO's general policy and future activities; decides to admit new member States and provides a world forum for the discussion of social and labour questions. Each national delegation to the Conference is composed of two Government delegates, one Employers' delegate and one Workers' delegate, accompanied as necessary by technical advisers. Employers' and Workers' delegates have a free voice; they can, and often do, disagree with their governments and with each other.

Along with the Declaration of Philadelphia, which is incorporated in the ILO Constitution, the Conference has in exceptional circumstances adopted other declarations of particular importance to ILO policy and action. A good example is the *Declaration concerning the Policy of Apartheid of the Republic of South Africa*, adopted in 1964 and later updated several times, in which the Conference condemns the policy of apartheid for being incompatible with the aims and objectives of the ILO, and sets out the lines of action to ensure respect for the freedom and dignity of all human beings, whatever their race. This Declaration was accompanied by a Programme of Action against Apartheid. Its application was the subject of a special report of the Director-General to the Conference each year on the economic and social situation in South Africa and on action taken against apartheid by governments, employers' and workers' organisations and by the international community. The Conference abrogated the Declaration in 1994. An ILO office has since been opened in the country, and the ILO is providing assistance in implementing new labour legislation. Its plan of action stresses the reinforcement of human and trade union rights, the establishment of employers' and workers' organisations, job creation, reform and restructuring of labour market institutions, and occupational safety and health.

It should be noted that four major international trade union organisations, namely the International Confederation of Free Trade Unions (ICFTU), the World Federation of Trade Unions (WFTU), the World Confederation of Labour (WCL) and the Organisation of African Trade Union Unity (OATUU), have full consultative status with the ILO. This means that they have the right to attend (but not to vote at) virtually any conference or meeting of any other body of the ILO. These organisations have an important advisory role to play in all ILO bodies, in particular through the Workers' group.

The Governing Body

The Governing Body is the executive council of the ILO and is elected every three years at the Conference. It is, so to speak, the hub of the wheel around which all ILO activities revolve. The Governing Body normally meets three times a year. It draws up the agenda for the Conference and other ILO meetings, takes note of their decisions and decides on the consequent action to be taken. It appoints the Director-General and directs the activities of the International Labour Office.

Like the Conference, the Governing Body is tripartite. It is currently composed of 56 voting members – 28 representing governments, 14 representing workers and 14 representing employers. Of the 28 government seats, ten are held by the States of chief industrial importance. The 18 other Government members are elected by the Government delegates at the International Labour Conference (other than those of chief industrial importance) who also elect 28 deputy Government members of the Governing Body. The Workers' delegates and the Employers' delegates at the Conference each elect 14 full members of the Governing Body as well as 19 deputy members.

The Governing Body plays an important role, as we shall see later, in the supervision and application of international labour standards. It has set up three bodies in particular for the protection of freedom of association – the Committee of Experts on the Application of Conventions and Recommendations (Chapter 6), the Fact-Finding and Conciliation Commission on Freedom of Association (Chapter 8), and the Governing Body Committee on Freedom of Association (Chapter 8).

The Governing Body may be called upon to set standards or social policy programmes on certain subjects when circumstances require it. Two texts of great importance to workers can be mentioned – the Tripartite Declaration of Principles on Multinational Enterprises and Social Policy, which is intended to provide guidance to governments, employers' and workers' organisations and multinational enterprises, and which it is recommended to be applied in the fields of employment, training, working and living conditions and industrial relations; and the International Programme for the Improvement of Working Conditions and Environment, which is designed to promote or support action by member States aimed at making work more human.

The Office

The International Labour Office in Geneva is the permanent secretariat of the ILO. It prepares the documents and reports which are the essential background material for the conferences and specialised meetings of the Organisation; provides the secretariat for these conferences and meetings; recruits technical co-operation experts and provides guidance for technical co-operation programmes throughout the world; engages in research and educational activities, collects information and statistics from all over the world across the whole spectrum of subjects relevant to the world of work (this provides, together with the ILO's own information and statistics, the basis for research and analysis which is then published through the ILO's books and periodicals); issues a broad range of specialised publications and periodicals dealing with labour and social matters; and assists government departments and employers' and workers' organisations. A number of regional ILO offices are located in various parts of the world.

Other components of the ILO structure

The preceding paragraphs have shown how the tripartite system of the ILO applies to the International Labour Conference and to the Governing Body. It should be added that the same system also applies to other ILO conferences.

Regional conferences bring together Government, Employers' and Workers' representatives of a specific region to study questions within the competence of the ILO of particular interest to that region, and to provide in-depth discussion. However, the regional conferences do not adopt international labour standards (Conventions and Recommendations), they do not have control over financial matters and they cannot decide to admit new member States.

The regional structure includes ILO regional offices located in Abidjan, Bangkok, Beirut, Lima and Geneva, and they are supported by 40 or so offices of the ILO in other countries. Thus, the ILO can maintain direct contacts with governments and with organisations of workers and employers. These offices in each region transmit information, advice and assistance to the three components of the ILO tripartite system in the respective region; and at the same time they ensure that the ILO is fully aware of current social problems, developments and policies in all the countries of the world.

Further, the ILO has strengthened its technical capacity by establishing 16 sub-regional multidisciplinary teams employing around 150 specialists. These services are thus much more accessible to the ILO's tripartite constituents in each member State, and the opportunities for increased dialogue and interaction are greatly enhanced.

Another noteworthy component of the ILO structure is its sectoral committees and meetings. These are tripartite or bipartite, and facilitate the exchange of views between ILO constituents on the problems faced in different economic sectors or branches of activity and on the solutions that may be found. The conclusions and/or resolutions which arise from these discussions between the social partners help to provide directions for policies and measures to be adopted at the national and international levels, as well as suggesting avenues for further ILO action and research in various economic sectors.

There are 22 sectoral committees in the following sectors:

(a) Industry:

— agriculture, plantations, other rural sectors;

— basic metal production;

— chemical industries;

— construction;

— food, drink, tobacco;

— forestry, wood, pulp and paper;

— mechanical and electrical engineering;

— mining (coal; other mining);

— oil and gas production; oil refining;

— textiles, clothing, leather, footwear;

— transport equipment manufacture.

(b) Maritime and transport:
— shipping, ports, fisheries, inland waterways;
— transport (including civil aviation, railways, road transport).

(c) Public and private services:
— commerce;
— education;
— financial services; professional services;
— health services;
— hotels, tourism, catering;
— media, culture, graphical;
— postal and other communication services;
— public services;
— utilities (water, gas, electricity).

On average, each sector is examined every four years by a meeting at the world level. During the intervening years, there may be regional and sub-regional meetings for the same sectors to allow the examination of particular issues at a more local level.

We must not forget to mention a number of other committees, commissions and groups of experts on various subjects. The Joint Maritime Commission is a bipartite body (composed of shipowners' and seafarers' representatives) which studies the working conditions of seafarers among other things and prepares the special (maritime) sessions of the International Labour Conference devoted to maritime questions.

The Joint Committee on the Public Service is also a bipartite body (composed of representatives of certain governments and civil service trade unions). A number of committees deal with specialised subjects, such as social security, rural development, health and safety. They advise the Governing Body on the questions referred to them. The important Committee of Experts on the Application of Conventions and Recommendations, as well as other bodies in the field of international labour standards, will be dealt with in detail in subsequent chapters. Certain joint committees of the ILO with other United Nations specialised agencies deal with matters of concern to the respective organisations. Such committees exist, for instance, with the Food and Agriculture

Organisation of the United Nations (FAO), the International Maritime Organisation (IMO), the United Nations Educational, Scientific and Cultural Organisation (UNESCO) and the World Health Organisation (WHO). Last but not least, various ad hoc meetings of experts are convened on a number of subjects.

The principle of tripartism

The unique strength of the International Labour Organisation comes from tripartism, which enables the representatives of workers and employers, alongside those of governments, to take part in all discussions and decision-making.

This active involvement of employers and workers side by side with governments, which constitutes the very essence of tripartism, also characterises every stage of the ILO's standard-setting activities. Subsequent chapters of this manual will illustrate in some detail the different forms that this active involvement may take. They will show how the origins of a Convention or a Recommendation may often be traced back to an initiative taken by a worker or a group of workers; how the Worker members in the Governing Body take part in determining the agenda of the International Labour Conference; how Workers' delegates to the Conference take part in the framing and adoption by the Conference of international labour standards; how workers' organisations have an important role to play both at the national and at the international level in monitoring the effective application of ratified Conventions; and how special complaints procedures are available to the workers where trade union rights are being violated or the terms of a ratified Convention are not being observed.

The success of this work largely depends on the extent to which workers and their organisations actively participate in the ILO's standard-setting work and actively make use of the rights conferred on them with a view to promoting a more effective and widespread application of ILO standards. The present manual will have served its purpose if it helps create among the workers an even greater awareness of the role that they can and should play in this regard.

It should also be emphasised that the principles of tripartism are reinforced by the Active Partnership Policy (see Chapter 6), which is aimed at strengthening the links between the ILO and its constituents in the design, implementation and follow-up of its action programmes.

Points for discussion

1. How and when did the ILO come into being? What are its basic principles and its main functions?
2. What do you think were the major problems facing workers in your country by 1919?
3. How did your country and your trade union movement participate in the founding and the early work of the ILO or in its activities in more recent years?
4. Describe the role and functions of the three main bodies of the International Labour Organisation: the International Labour Conference, the Governing Body and the International Labour Office.

Group exercise

Form three groups representing governments, workers and employers: discuss an issue which could be put before the International Labour Conference or the Governing Body for consideration and decision; and then vote according to the voting rules of the ILO and compare how each group has voted on the subject. The voting system for the International Labour Conference is based on each member State having four delegates: two representing the government, and one each for employers and workers. Each delegate has one vote and the right to vote as an individual, regardless of the way other members of the national delegation vote.

On balance, were the results to the advantage or disadvantage of the workers?

Further reading

Antony Alcock: *History of the International Labour Organisation*, London, Macmillan, and New York, Octagon Books, 1971.

E.J. Phelan: *Yes and Albert Thomas*, New York, Columbia University Press, 1949.

ILO: *Trade unions and the ILO*, A workers' education manual, second (revised) edition, Geneva, 1988.

ILO: *The ILO in the service of social progress*, A workers' education manual, second (revised) edition, Geneva, 1995.

Chapter 2

How international labour standards originate

Everything must start somewhere; but it is normally as difficult and time-consuming to find out who originally had the idea or ideas underlying any ILO Convention or Recommendation as it is to find the proverbial needle in a haystack. It may be the man or woman on the job; their doctor; the employer; a trade union official; a government official – almost anybody. However, since ILO standards usually deal with issues common to most workers, or to large categories of workers, in many or in all member States, most of the ideas have probably occurred to several people in a number of countries at just about the same time. Mostly these are workers who come with a suggestion to regulate by international labour legislation an issue of concern to them.

What is essential, if the idea as first formulated is to be converted into a labour standard, is that it will be passed on to somebody who knows how to feed it into the ILO system. There are various ways in which this can be done, but a few typical examples will be sufficient to illustrate the general principles involved. As already mentioned in the first chapter, the agenda of the International Labour Conference is drawn up by the Governing Body of the ILO. The agenda includes items relating to the drawing up of new Conventions and Recommendations. The idea must therefore first reach the Governing Body, and be proposed for inclusion on the Conference agenda by one of the three groups of Governing Body members, namely the representatives of governments, workers or employers.

Once an idea is conceived by a worker on the job, the route that it has to travel will depend very much on the conditions prevailing in the particular country – for example, the way in which the trade unions are organised and the ease of communication between trade unions, government and employers. It may also depend on the international affiliations of the trade unions in the particular country.

Once the idea goes, from a worker or a group of workers to reach the national trade union level, however, several possibilities are usually open. One approach may be for the union to get in touch with the government and to explore the possibilities of a joint move or at least to obtain the government's backing. At the same time, or alternatively, the union may request the international trade union federation to which it belongs to take up the matter. In this case the international federation may arrange for the Workers' group on the ILO Governing Body to raise the subject in the Governing Body. Otherwise the national trade union organisation, sometimes in co-operation with one or more friendly trade unions from other countries, may formulate the idea into a document to be directed to and subsequently considered by the ILO. Such a document is normally prepared in co-operation with the international trade union body to which the national trade unions concerned are affiliated. The usual kind of document is a resolution which is submitted to the International Labour Conference by a delegate. However, such an initiative may also come through other ILO bodies, such as regional conferences, meetings of Industrial Committees and tripartite technical conferences. The conclusions, recommendations or resolutions of these bodies are submitted to the Governing Body for decision as to what action should be taken on them.

In this connection, it might be appropriate to recall that four major international trade union organisations, namely the ICFTU, the WFTU, the WCL and the OATUU have full consultative status with the ILO. This means that they have the right to attend (but not to vote at) any meeting of ILO bodies, and to participate actively in them, as well as in any other activity of the ILO. They are particularly involved in the various aspects of the standard-setting activities and the supervisory system.

Many resolutions adopted by the International Labour Conference, frequently on the initiative of one or more Workers' delegates to the Conference, contain requests that the Governing Body should place a particular matter on the agenda of the Conference with a view to the adoption of one or more international labour Conventions or Recommendations. Thus, the adoption in 1975 of a new international Convention concerning the protection of migrant workers, and of a Recommendation on the same subject, was the result of resolutions submitted in 1971 and 1972 by a number of Workers' delegates; and the adoption in 1976 of a Convention and a Recommendation concerning tripartite consultations to improve the application (or "implementation") of ILO standards was the result of action taken on a 1971 Conference resolution that had also been submitted by several Workers' delegates.

There are many variations on the methods described above, and they cannot all be dealt with here. Most proposals for new or improved labour standards have come from the labour movement, but it should be mentioned that employers, governments, the International Labour Office, ILO Industrial Committees and a number of other bodies have also been responsible for their share. On top of that the United Nations can refer some issues to the ILO for action, and that action may lead to the adoption of international labour standards.

Examples

Before going on to a more detailed analysis of the subsequent stages that an unborn Convention must go through before it is adopted by the International Labour Conference, it may be useful to take a look at a few existing Conventions and see in what form the ideas (or the problems to which they relate) first reached the ILO.

Freedom of association

The first international Convention specifically concerned with freedom of association was the Right of Association (Agriculture) Convention, 1921 (No. 11), which required ratifying States to secure "to all those engaged in agriculture the same rights of association and combination as to industrial workers". The object, obviously, was to remove an inequality. The Convention did not by itself guarantee any basic freedom, since "the same rights" might be no rights at all, or rights that were severely circumscribed.

As a result, it soon became clear that freedom of association could be effectively safeguarded only by a Convention applicable to all workers and defining their rights in precise terms. During the period between the two world wars several attempts were made to secure the adoption of a Convention embodying a clear-cut obligation to give effect to the principle of freedom of association, set forth in the ILO's Constitution. These attempts failed, however. In part, this was due to differences of opinion on the contents of the proposed Convention, for instance on whether freedom of association should comprise not only the right to organise but also the right not to do so. Essentially, however, the difficulties were of a political nature, linked to the fact that totalitarian regimes had sprung up in a number of European countries, as well as in other continents, which had either suppressed employers' and workers' organisations or reduced them to a subordinate position.

After the Second World War, the workers' organisations took up the question again. On 14 January 1947 the WFTU dispatched a letter to the Secretary-General of the United Nations, requesting that "guarantees for the exercise and development of trade union rights" be considered by the Economic and Social Council. Enclosed with the letter was the text of a draft resolution which, among other things, required the Council to set up a permanent "committee for trade union rights". Before this, in August 1946, the American Federation of Labor (AF of L), which was not a member of the WFTU, had circulated an alternative text to members of the Council. The principal difference between the WFTU and the AF of L proposals was that the latter required the Economic and Social Council to delegate responsibility for freedom of association to the ILO, instead of creating its own committee for trade union rights. However, both texts called for some sort of international convention.

Towards the end of 1945, the United Nations and the International Labour Organisation had entered into an agreement. The first article of the agreement recognises the ILO's responsibility for matters covered by its Constitution, and the third gives each organisation the right to request that items be placed on the agenda of the other. When the Economic and Social Council met in March 1947 to consider the WFTU and AF of L proposals, it decided by a majority vote to send both documents to the ILO, with a request that the question be placed on the agenda of its next session "and that a report be sent to the Economic and Social Council for its consideration at the next meeting of the Council". The question was discussed by the International Labour Conference in June 1947, and led to the adoption in 1948 of the Freedom of Association and Protection of the Right to Organise Convention (No. 87). This is a good example of how new labour standards can result when the United Nations refers matters to the ILO; but it is worth noticing that it was the trade unions that started the ball rolling in the first place.

Protection of wages

When the International Labour Conference met in Philadelphia in 1944 it had before it a report prepared by the Office which contained the draft of the Declaration of Philadelphia. The report also contained recommendations for future action by the ILO. Among other things it pointed out that wage policy lay "at the core of the preoccupations of the International Labour Organisation"; yet, up to that time, only three international standards touching on the subject had been adopted. The report stated:

> A Convention or Recommendation on methods of wage payment dealing with the periodicity of wage payments, deductions from wages, the prohibition of truck (the obligation to spend wages on goods supplied by the employers), the adequacy of remuneration in kind, the protection of wages in legal proceedings and similar subjects would also be of great value in relation to many parts of the world, especially in regard to rural workers.

This was the germ of the Protection of Wages Convention, 1949 (No. 95).

In this case it was the International Labour Office itself which initiated a Convention by means of an Office report.

Crew accommodation

Conditions of work at sea have been a major concern of the ILO since its inception. A Joint Maritime Commission of workers' and employers' representatives – no governments – was formed in 1920, and special maritime sessions of the International Labour Conference have been held at intervals since that year.

During the Second World War the International Transport Workers' Federation (to which seafarers' unions are affiliated) and the International Mercantile Marine Officers' Association jointly issued an international seamen's charter, which they submitted to the Joint Maritime Commission of the ILO. One of the points covered in the charter was crew accommodation. In January 1945 the Joint Maritime Commission recommended that a special maritime session of the International Labour Conference should be convened. In the meantime, preparatory technical meetings, with government representatives taking part, should prepare drafts covering various aspects of the working conditions of seamen. This was the beginning of the process which culminated, in 1946, in the adoption of no fewer than nine Conventions[1] and four Recommendations[2] for the protection of seafarers. One of them was the Accommodation of Crews Convention (No. 75).

Ratifications of this Convention were disappointingly few. Several governments indicated that they would be happy to ratify the Convention if certain points could be clarified. The workers insisted that, whatever the way out of the difficulty, effective standards should not be lowered. In the end a tripartite subcommittee of the Joint Maritime Commission looked at the text again, and in due course the Accommodation of Crews Convention (Revised), 1949 (No. 92), came into existence, thanks to the interest taken in the matter by the international organisations representing the seafarers.[3]

Guarding of machinery

As long ago as 1929, the ILO adopted the Power-driven Machinery Recommendation (No. 32) which called on member States to "apply to as great an extent as possible the principle that it should be prohibited by law to supply or install any machine intended to be driven by mechanical power and to be used within its territory, unless it is furnished with the safety appliances required by law for the operation of machines of that type". The text did not have the force of a Convention, and it did not specify which parts of the machinery in question should be considered particularly dangerous; that depended on national laws. In this respect, the Recommendation did not in fact lay down international standards. Another Recommendation, the Prevention of Industrial Accidents Recommendation, 1929 (No. 31), was concerned with accident statistics, research and the organisation of industrial safety services; it, too, did not enter into the techniques of accident prevention.

The problems of machine guards are more complex than it may seem at first sight. At the time when a machine is sold, and certainly at the time when it is designed, it may be impossible to say just how it will be used;

indeed, it may not always be used for the same purpose. Some of the most dangerous parts, such as cutting tools, may not be permanent fixtures. In 1956 a panel of experts appointed by the ILO was instructed to study the matter. In simple terms, what they had to decide was whether there were certain basic sources of danger which could be identified before a machine was sold, and to what extent there was a need for more detailed standards on the subject.

The panel recommended that a Convention be drafted prohibiting the sale, hire and use of unguarded machinery. In due course, the Governing Body placed the question on the Conference agenda. This resulted in the adoption in 1963 of the Guarding of Machinery Convention (No. 119) and Recommendation (No. 118).

This was a case in which occupational safety specialists came up with proposals for extending international standards, after they had agreed that a further step forward had become technically feasible.

Safe use of asbestos

The protection of health against the harmful effects resulting from exposure to asbestos dusts (mainly causing asbestosis and several types of cancer) became, after the Second World War, a subject of great concern not only for workers' organisations, but also for employers' organisations, the competent national prevention services and the public at large. The world production of asbestos increased greatly to reach 5 million tons in 1974 (compared with some 675,000 tons in 1940) and to exceed 6 million tons in 1980. Thus the number of workers exposed to asbestos has considerably increased. Moreover, the risk of asbestos-related diseases has extended much beyond the industries directly concerned; the presence of asbestos in the environment in certain regions of the world has reached the point where it appears to pose a health hazard for the population as a whole.

In November 1972, when considering the occupational safety and health programme of the ILO (as a part of the programme and budget of the ILO for 1972-73), the Governing Body decided to hold a meeting of experts on the safe use of asbestos. The Workers' group of the Governing Body was pushing strongly for this meeting, which took place in December 1973. It identified the pathological effects of exposure to asbestos and suggested a number of measures to improve the protection of workers and to reduce hazards to a minimum. It also recommended the adoption of an international instrument on the subject, as well as the elaboration of a guide on the safe use of asbestos, in consultation with appropriate national and international bodies.

In June 1980, the International Labour Conference adopted a new list of occupational diseases appended to the Employment Injury Benefits Convention, 1964 (No. 121), in which lung cancer caused by asbestos was included. Asbestosis had already been covered by the original list.

In November 1980, the Governing Body decided to call another meeting of experts, which was convened in October 1981. The experts made recommendations on the content of an international instrument and suggested to the Governing Body the elaboration of a code of practice which would either precede the instrument or proceed in parallel.

In February-March 1982, the Governing Body called for a third meeting of experts on the safe use of asbestos. This meeting, which took place in October 1983, drew up a Code of Practice on Safety in the Use of Asbestos. At its session in November 1983, the Governing Body took note of this code and authorised the Director-General of the ILO to publish it. At the same time, the Governing Body decided to place on the agenda of the 71st Session of the International Labour Conference in 1985 the question of safety in the use of asbestos. The subject was dealt with by the Conference under the double-discussion procedure (i.e. at two subsequent sessions, in 1985 and 1986) and in 1986 the Conference adopted the Asbestos Convention (No. 162) and Recommendation (No. 172).

Other cases

While the first move may come from any of the three partners in the ILO – workers, employers or governments – the foregoing examples show that the initiative can more often than not be traced to the trade unions. This is not surprising. It is after all the workers who benefit directly from international labour standards. However, there are other possibilities as well.

Sometimes when a problem is of special concern to a number of organisations in the United Nations system they may decide to act jointly. The Radiation Protection Convention, 1960 (No. 115), for example, was developed by the ILO in close collaboration with the International Atomic Energy Agency (IAEA) and the World Health Organisation (WHO), and the Indigenous and Tribal Populations Convention, 1957 (No. 107), with the co-operation of the United Nations, the FAO, UNESCO and the WHO. Conversely, the ILO may play a part in the initiation of an international Convention or Recommendation adopted by a sister organisation. A case in point is the Recommendation concerning the status of teachers which was adopted by UNESCO in 1966, and is sometimes called the Teachers' Charter.

Notes

[1] Nos. 68-76.

[2] Nos. 75-78.

[3] A further Convention on the same subject, the Accommodation of Crews (Supplementary Provisions) Convention, was adopted in 1970.

Points for discussion

1. Describe the role of workers in shaping international labour standards.
2. In what forms and ways may workers take the initiative to adopt an ILO instrument (Convention, Recommendation)?
3. Has your organisation already had some experience with an initiative (either through a resolution or otherwise) which has led to the adoption of an international labour instrument?

Group exercise

Identify and discuss a specific issue concerning the interests of workers, and identify the successive steps that would have to be taken with a view to obtaining a decision on the matter by the International Labour Conference. If appropriate for such a discussion, form groups representing the trade union branch, the national union, the international trade union organisation, the government (or even the employers), the Governing Body of the ILO and the International Labour Conference.

Further reading

ILO: *Trade unions and the ILO*, A workers' education manual, second (revised) edition, Geneva, 1988.

ILO: *Trade union participation in shaping and adopting international labour standards*, course topic, Geneva, 1994, available from the Bureau for Workers' Activities.

Chapter 3

The standard-setting process

We have now reached the stage when the idea or problem that started the whole process has taken a more definite form and has become a subject which the Governing Body has chosen for possible inclusion in the agenda of the International Labour Conference, with a view to adopting a Convention or a Recommendation or both (see figure 1).

The procedure

The first step along the way is that – at the Governing Body's request – the secretariat, i.e. the International Labour Office, prepares a comparative study of the laws and practices relating to the subject in the various member States. This is a complicated task, not just because of the large number of member States, but also because many of the subjects covered by ILO standards are highly technical. This again means that from this point up to the adoption of the standard, everything usually has to be done by a team which, apart from legal experts, will include experts on the technical aspects of the subject.

On the basis of this law-and-practice report the Governing Body makes the final decision on whether or not to go ahead with the standard-setting process. If the answer is "yes", a more detailed law-and-practice report and the outline of a possible text are prepared by the Office, the latter in questionnaire form. These are sent to the member States not less than a year before the start of the session of the Conference at which the item is to be discussed. The governments' answers must be sent to the ILO at least eight months before the Conference meets. In preparing their answers, governments are expected to consult workers' and employers' organisations; and many of them in fact do this although it is not compulsory. The only governments that are bound to tripartite consultations and must therefore consult workers' and employers' organisations at this stage are those which have ratified the Tripartite Consultation (International Labour Standards) Convention, 1976 (No. 144). This Convention and its accompanying Recommendation represent a major step forward in the history of ILO standard-setting, and more will be said about this in a later chapter. It should be recalled in this connection that on the basis of the resolution concerning the strengthening of tripartism in the overall activities of the ILO, adopted by the Conference at its 56th Session (1971), the Governing Body at its 183rd Session in June 1971 addressed to governments a recommendation that they "consult the most representative organisations of employers and workers before they finalise replies to the ILO questionnaires".

On the basis of governments' replies, the Office prepares a set of proposed conclusions which in reality is the first draft of the proposed text. It is sent to governments four months before the beginning of the Conference. And again governments are expected to consult workers' and employers' organisations. The scene is now set for the first discussion by the Conference. When the Conference meets, it normally appoints a tripartite committee to examine the proposals. The committee, on which voting rights are weighted so as to ensure equality between the representatives of governments, employers and workers, makes such changes in the text as are thought necessary by its members. The agreed text is then submitted to the full Conference, together with a resolution placing the question on the agenda of the Conference the following year, with a view to the adoption, at that time, of the proposed Convention or Recommendation or both. Things can go wrong at this stage if the committee fails to reach a fair measure of agreement, or if the Conference as a whole fails to adopt the resolution, but in normal circumstances the original problem is now well under way to becoming the subject of an international labour standard.

After this first Conference discussion, the Office drafts a provisional text of the proposed Convention and/or Recommendation, and sends it to governments within two months of the closing of the Conference session. Governments have three months in which to submit amendments or make other suggestions. They should again consult workers' and employers' organisations. The Office then prepares a final report and sends it to the governments at least three months before the next session of the Conference is due to meet. It normally sends the report to trade union organisations as well. At the Conference, the draft is again examined by a tripartite committee and the agreed text put before the full Conference for approval. If it receives two-thirds of the votes cast it is formally adopted as an ILO Convention and/or Recommendation.

There are some exceptions to the use of this double-discussion procedure, i.e. discussion of the matter at two successive sessions of the Conference,

Figure 1. Process of adoption of international labour standards (Conventions and Recommendations) – (most often at the initiative of workers, and culminating in a resolution adopted at the International Labour Conference)

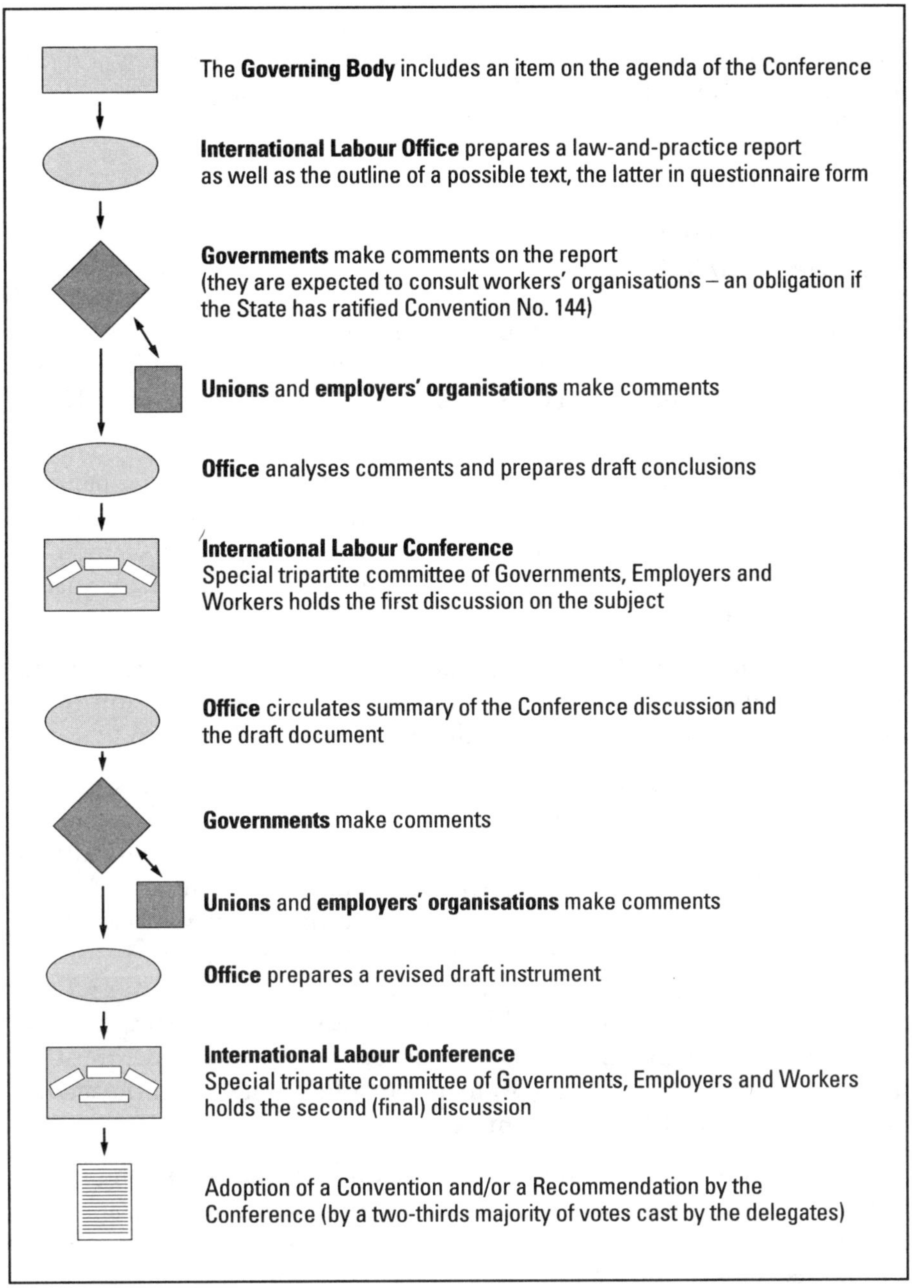

are "in cases of special urgency or where other special circumstances exist", when the Governing Body may decide by a three-fifths majority on a single discussion. The main exceptions have in the past related to maritime standards and other cases where there has already been a preliminary technical meeting, and to revised standards when the revised text follows the original Convention or Recommendation fairly closely.

A case history

A good way to illustrate the procedure is to take a look at the Guarding of Machinery Convention, 1963, which was mentioned in the preceding chapter. Its history is fairly typical and can briefly be summarised as follows:

June 1959-May 1960: On the basis of a report submitted by a panel of experts, the Governing Body instructed the Director-General to submit an Office report concerning the law and practice in ILO member States on the prohibition of the sale, hire and use of inadequately guarded machinery.

November 1960: The Governing Body studied the Office report and decided to place the question on the agenda of the 46th Session of the International Labour Conference, due to be held in June 1962.

May 1961: A preparatory report was circulated to governments. It contained relevant accident statistics from several countries, a survey of the technical points, a brief discussion of feasible international controls, an outline of the proposed ILO instrument and a questionnaire. An 18-page appendix reviewed the law and practice in 22 different countries. Governments were requested to reply to the questionnaire before 30 September 1961. (It was not until 1971 that the Governing Body decided that governments should always be asked to "consult the most representative organisations of employers and workers before they finalise replies to the ILO questionnaires relating to items on the agenda of the International Labour Conference".)

January 1962: The Office distributed a second report comprising replies from 77 countries to the questionnaire, a brief commentary, and proposed conclusions specifying the points of substance to be included in a proposed Convention and in a Recommendation.

June 1962: The International Labour Conference appointed a tripartite committee on unguarded machinery. The committee met 17 times, producing a report which concluded with a revised draft of the proposed conclusions. The report was discussed and adopted by the Conference on 27 June, and the question was placed on the agenda of the next session of the Conference.

August 1962: This report, as adopted by the Conference and including the draft texts of the Convention and Recommendation, was then sent to governments, who were asked to comment by 30 November 1962.

February 1963: The Office circulated a final report analysing the comments of governments having responded to this request.

June 1963: The International Labour Conference appointed a tripartite committee on guarding of machinery, which met 14 times and discussed 57 proposed amendments. The final texts of a Convention and a Recommendation were presented to the Conference on 22 June, and both instruments were adopted unanimously.

Basic issues

We have now familiarised ourselves with the successive steps and procedures that lead up to the adoption of a Convention or Recommendation, and have seen how at each stage of this lengthy process – from the placing of an item on the agenda of the International Labour Conference to the final voting by the Conference in plenary session – workers and employers have a fundamentally important role to play alongside with governments. This truly is tripartism in action. In subsequent chapters we shall be examining the steps and procedures that may lead to the ratification of a Convention or the acceptance of a Recommendation, and the supervisory system that has been developed over the years with a view to ensuring that ratified Conventions are effectively implemented or that governments otherwise comply with their obligations under the ILO Constitution with regard to international labour standards. There, too, particular emphasis will be laid on the role and responsibilities of workers and employers.

This is, however, an appropriate moment at which to pause and consider briefly a few issues of basic importance that have faced (and continue to face) the ILO with regard to its standard-setting action. They are issues which in recent years have been much discussed, both at the International Labour Conference and in the ILO Governing Body, the latter having devoted considerable attention to these questions in a so-called "in-depth review" of international labour standards, established in 1974.

Flexibility

International labour standards are intended to be universal in nature, i.e. applicable to and capable of attainment by countries with very different social structures and at all stages of industrial development. To attain this objective, standards should be flexible rather than rigid, but must at the same time set meaningful targets for social development. Is this an exercise in squaring the circle, or can it be done?

Article 19, paragraph 3, of the ILO Constitution provides that "in framing any Convention or Recommendation of general application the Conference shall have due regard to those countries in which climatic conditions, the imperfect development of industrial organisation, or other special circumstances make the industrial conditions substantially different and shall suggest the modifications, if any, which it considers may be required to meet the case of such countries". Systematic efforts are made in the standard-setting process to give effect to this constitutional directive. When the discussion of an item on the agenda of the Conference is intended to lead to the adoption of standards, the initial report submitted to the Conference always includes a special passage drawing attention to the importance of ensuring the necessary flexibility to take account of national peculiarities; the questionnaire appearing at the end of the report contains a special question asking for information and suggestions in this respect.

The results of this approach may be illustrated by the new standards on minimum age for admission to employment, adopted in 1973. In the first place, these standards were separated into a Convention (No. 138) and a supplementary Recommendation (No. 146). The Convention starts with a commitment to a general policy to abolish child labour and progressively to raise the minimum age for employment. Its application may initially be limited to specified sectors of activity. The general minimum age level to be accepted upon ratification may be 15 years or, for countries whose economy and educational facilities are insufficiently developed, 14 years. Limited light work – in activities to be prescribed by the national authorities – may be permitted for young persons between 13 and 15 years of age or, in less developed countries, between 12 and 14 years. It is left to the authorities in each country to determine the dangerous or unhealthy occupations to which a higher minimum age should apply, and this age – while generally 18 years may under certain conditions also be fixed at 16 years. Limited categories of workers in respect of whom special and substantial difficulties of application arise may be excluded from the Convention. It also permits the granting of individual exceptions for certain purposes. While the Convention thus leaves a considerable measure of discretion to national authorities, it establishes certain procedural guarantees: in most cases the decisions of the authorities must be preceded by consultation of employers' and workers' organisations; the exception clauses also generally require governments to indicate in their reports on the application of the Convention any developments towards its fuller acceptance, and provide for the possibility of cancelling any exception.

The question of flexibility of standards has been reviewed on a number of occasions by the ILO, especially within the context of the in-depth review of standards referred to earlier in this chapter as well as of reports in 1979 and 1987 by working parties on international labour standards established by the Governing Body. A new working party, the Working Party on Policy regarding the Revision of Standards, established in 1995, is looking at the whole policy of standard-setting and revision of all standards except the fundamental human rights Conventions. Its work was continuing in 1998. The essential conclusions emerging from these documents were that an international standard which is unduly rigid will not serve as a target for national action and that standards must represent realistic targets for countries at different levels of development, while particularly ensuring that they are adapted to the special needs of developing countries. The ILO has approved and developed a wide range of flexibility devices aimed at enabling the greatest number of States progressively to ensure the intended protection. These devices include, in particular, the possibility of accepting a Convention in parts; the possibility of excluding certain sectors of activity, categories of workers or areas of the country from its scope; "escalator" clauses making possible the gradual raising of the level of protection or the extension of the scope of protection; the adoption of Conventions which lay down only basic principles, more precise and detailed standards being incorporated in a supplementary Recommendation; the possibility of adopting alternative solutions to a problem; and flexibility in the methods of application.

In more concrete terms, the problem is to ensure that ILO standards represent meaningful and practicable targets for both more developed and less developed countries. The foregoing summary of the various flexibility devices embodied in the minimum age instruments shows the approach followed in dealing with the problem. Another particularly striking example is provided by the Conventions on social security. For instance, the Social Security (Minimum Standards) Convention, 1952 (No. 102), permits ratification in respect of as few as three out of a list of nine types of benefits (covering such contingencies as sickness, unemployment, maternity or old age) and also enables countries "whose economy and medical facilities are insufficiently developed" to make certain temporary exceptions in regard to such matters as the proportion of protected persons and the duration of benefits. In a number of instances, standards have been framed with special regard to the needs of these countries; examples are the Recommendations on co-operatives in developing countries (No. 127), tenants and sharecroppers (No. 132), and special youth employment and training schemes (No. 136), parts of the Employment Policy Recommendation (No. 122), and the Minimum Wage Fixing Convention (No. 131) and Recommendation (No. 135).

Another example is the Occupational Health Services Convention, 1985 (No. 161), supplemented by a Recommendation (No. 171). The Convention permits (and, analogously, the Recommendation recommends) the progressive development of occupational health services for all workers. Member States which are not in a position to establish such services immediately in all enterprises are invited to draw up plans for their establishment, in consultation with the most representative organisations of employers and workers. A further method that is often used in order to achieve the necessary degree of flexibility is to lay down only the basic principles in a Convention, which is then supplemented by more precise and detailed standards in a Recommendation. This method has in fact been used in over 60 cases. The Employment Policy Convention (No. 122) and Recommendation (No. 122), 1964, provide a good example of this approach: the obligation assumed by a State which ratifies the Convention is "to declare and pursue, as a major goal, an active policy designed to promote full, productive and freely chosen employment"; on the other hand, the means by which such a policy should be pursued are spelt out in considerable detail in the accompanying Recommendation.

In connection with the flexibility of international labour standards it might be recalled that Workers' members of the Working Party on

International Labour Standards, established by the Governing Body in November 1984, felt somehow uneasy about the very concept of flexibility, mostly because it was open to different interpretations. They pointed out that the resulting uncertainty might to some extent account for the limited recourse by member States to the flexibility clauses included in certain Conventions. On the other band, they stressed that there was no scope for flexibility in Conventions on fundamental human rights and basic freedoms.

Regional or universal standards?

This brings us to a related question of considerable importance. Is there scope, and if so to what extent, for the adoption of standards applicable only to a given region rather than standards of a universal character? The matter has been raised from time to time in the past and was also considered in the context of the in-depth review of, and working parties on, international labour standards referred to above. Broadly speaking, however, and in spite of the fact that many problems in a given region are frequently of a similar character, there has always emerged a general agreement in favour of the continued setting of standards on a worldwide basis, provided that such standards are given the necessary degree of flexibility and that they are conceived so as to respond to the needs of all member States.

Promotional Conventions

A word or two should also be said about a trend in the standard-setting work of the ILO that is becoming increasingly noticeable. ILO Conventions originally contained relatively precise standards that could be taken over directly into national legislation. Since the Second World War another kind of text has come into being, namely the so-called "promotional" Convention, whereby individual ratifying States undertake to pursue stated objectives, but by methods that are left largely to their own discretion, as is the timing of the changes made. There can, of course, be no doubt of the value of such a legal commitment where the objective is defined with precision, and where progress towards its attainment can be measured with a fair amount of certainty. From this point of view, promotional Conventions such as the Equal Remuneration Convention, 1951 (No. 100), and the Discrimination (Employment and Occupation) Convention, 1958 (No. 111), have undoubtedly had a considerable effect in many countries. In other cases, in which the aim may be less easy to define with clarity, objective evaluation of the extent of compliance with the international commitment becomes difficult, and the use of the Convention form becomes more open to doubt: in such cases it might be preferable to cast proposed standards in the form of Recommendations, enjoying the authority of internationally accepted principles of social policy, but not involving a formal legal commitment in the event of ratification.

In this connection, it is important to comment upon the participation of workers' and employers' organisations in the process of giving effect to the provisions of ILO instruments. The promotional Conventions in particular, but also a considerable number of other instruments, especially those adopted in recent years, contain many provisions requiring tripartite involvement in their implementation at the national level. The governments themselves are requested to seek workers' and employers' participation.

The degree or kind of participation varies. The Workers with Family Responsibilities Convention, 1981 (No. 156), for instance, specifies that. "Employers' and workers' organisations shall have the right to participate, in a manner appropriate to national conditions and practice, in devising and applying measures designed to give effect to the provisions of this Convention." Measures taken by public authorities to give effect to the Collective Bargaining Convention, 1981 (No. 154), are subject to prior consultation and, whenever possible, agreement between the public authorities and employers' and workers' organisations. An agreement, or at least full consultation, with the representative organisations of workers and employers is required for the implementation of the Minimum Wage Fixing Convention, 1970 (No. 131). This Convention also provides for the direct participation in its operation of representatives of the employers' and workers' organisations concerned.

Conventions or Recommendations?

The basic difference between these two forms of standard is that a Convention is designed to be ratified, like an international treaty; a ratifying State undertakes to discharge certain binding legal obligations, and there is regular international supervision of the way in which those obligations are observed. A Recommendation, on the other hand, gives rise to no binding obligations but provides guide-lines for national policies and action. Essentially for this reason, Workers' delegates to the International Labour Conference often press for the adoption of a Convention whereas the Employers' delegates are more in favour of a Recommendation.

The matter is necessarily one of judgement, and the dilemma was already recognised by the commission on international labour legislation in 1919. In a report to the peace conference the commission stated:

> Subjects will probably come before the Conference [the International Labour Conference] which, owing to their complexity and the wide differences in the circumstances of different countries, will be incapable of being reduced to any universal and uniform mode of application. In such cases a Convention might prove impossible, but a Recommendation of principles in more or less detail which left the individual States freedom to apply them in the manner best suited to their conditions would undoubtedly have considerable value.

That is still true in some cases. However, that approach is now rare. It might be recalled that while in the period from 1951 to 1970 well over half of the Recommendations adopted (i.e. 31 out of 55) were autonomous instruments unrelated to a Convention, from 1971 to 1997 only three out of 46 Recommendations have been of this nature, the remainder all being instruments supplementing a Convention.

Another form of instrument sometimes adopted is the Protocol. This is effectively a partial revision of a Convention. Of the four adopted by 1997, two (those to Conventions Nos. 89 and 110) aimed to introduce greater flexibility into the principal Conventions; the others (to Conventions Nos. 81 and 147) allow States which ratify them to extend their obligations under the principal Conventions.

This manual will show that many of the procedures developed by the ILO in order to promote effective application of its international labour standards apply not only to Conventions but also to Recommendations; that under the Constitution of the ILO both Conventions and Recommendations must be brought before the appropriate body in each member State "for the enactment of legislation or other action"; that in respect of both, each member State must report on the action taken; and that in respect of both, there is an obligation to submit further reports, though admittedly at less frequent and regular intervals in the case of Recommendations than in that of Conventions.

What, then, has been the attitude of the International Labour Conference when faced with this choice? It is often a difficult one to make. Broadly speaking, it can perhaps be said that the Conference has found precise questions of conditions of employment (hours of work, minimum wages, holidays with pay), of safety and health, of social security and of human rights to be suitable for Conventions. On the other hand, it has chosen Recommendations in cases where the subject has not yet been considered ripe for a Convention because it is more or less new and the standards more or less exploratory; where an agreed aim can be achieved by a variety of methods and the Conference has wanted to leave a measure of freedom for national action; where the Conference has considered it undesirable to overload a Convention with detailed guide-lines on the application of the principles it lays down; or where the Conference has wanted to set as a target for development a standard which, if contained in a Convention, would receive only few ratifications in the foreseeable future. In the two last-mentioned cases, what normally happens is that the Conference adopts both a Convention and an accompanying Recommendation at the same time.

Future standards

As the workers' representatives on various ILO bodies have observed on a number of occasions, ILO standards must constitute a basis for the social action of member States. They should set goals to attain in the future and point the direction in which social progress should move. Governments should draw inspiration from standards in setting targets for social progress in their countries. Workers are, therefore, in favour of continuing to elaborate standards, without any slowing down in the pace of standard setting. This trend was clearly shown by the large number of items identified in the classification as possible subjects for new or revised standards, established by the Working Party on International Labour Standards and approved by the Governing Body in 1979.

At its session in March 1987 the Governing Body discussed and approved the revised classification (established by another Working Party on International Labour Standards) of existing Conventions and Recommendations and noted possible subjects for new standards. The discussion reflected varying opinions by various countries and by the Workers' and Employers' groups in the ILO as regards the general policy regarding ILO standard-setting activities. While there is very broad agreement on the value of these activities and on the universality of standards (responding to the needs of all member States), no agreement has been reached as regards the conditions in which the standard-setting activities should be carried out. There are suggestions to give priority to the implementation of existing standards rather than the adoption of new instruments; to slow the pace of standard setting in order to improve quality; to use more Recommendations as instruments in their own right rather than merely appendages to Conventions; to continue to elaborate standards, but primarily those relating to human rights.

Standard setting will in the future certainly continue to be an important aspect of the work of the ILO, important above all for workers. Standards will have to be framed in such a manner that most countries will face no difficulty in ratifying them in the foreseeable future. Particular care should be taken not to transform illusions into standards, for in that case standards would forever remain illusions.

The need for revisions

There is now a consensus on the need to revise certain Conventions. The Workers' group believe that an objective examination of Conventions should precede any revision, and that this should in no way hinder the system of standards or the adoption of new instruments. They consider that a low level of ratification for a given Convention does not necessarily mean that revision is needed. They have, however, recognised that revision could be justified if there is agreement among the ILO's tripartite constituents on the difficulty of ratifying a Convention because certain dispositions presented problems. Further, the Workers have laid down four preconditions concerning partial or total revisions: that they should not be used to reduce the protection afforded to workers; that there is a climate of confidence among the three groups; that the revisions are based on in-depth analysis; and that consensus can emerge on the identification of serious problems that ratification could pose to certain States, which cannot be resolved by the supervisory bodies. In the Conference Committee on the Application of Conventions and Recommendations a consensus has been expressed on the need to organise a general discussion at the Conference before elaborating or revising a standard. The Governing Body set up the Working Party on Policy regarding the Revision of Standards in 1995. At each session of the Governing Body, the Working Party reports on the progress of its work regarding the need to revise standards studied on a case-by-case basis. Some Conventions already include specific clauses intended to simplify the revision of certain dispositions, such as the Employment Injury Benefits Convention, 1964 (No. 121), Schedule I of which was amended in 1980. Revision sometimes raises the problem of overlap between Conventions remaining in force, even though they have a new text. Two-thirds of the revisions so far have been on three subjects: minimum age, social security and seafarers.

Points for discussion

1. Describe the various stages of the standard-setting process.
2. What do you understand by the flexibility of international labour standards? How is this flexibility achieved?
3. What is the role of promotional Conventions? Discuss some recent examples of such Conventions.
4. What kind of instrument do you prefer: Conventions or Recommendations?
5. Give an example – if possible – from your own participation as a workers' representative in the procedure for shaping and adopting international labour standards.

Group exercise

Identify a subject meriting the formulation and adoption of an international labour instrument. Form three groups (representing governments, workers and employers at the International Labour Conference) to discuss the formulation of the main ideas into the instrument.

Further reading

ILO: *Trade unions and the ILO*, A workers' education manual, second (revised) edition, Geneva, 1988.

ILO: *Trade union participation in shaping and adopting international labour standards*, course topic, Geneva, 1994, available from the Bureau for Workers' Activities.

Report of the Working Party on International Labour Standards, *Official Bulletin of the ILO*, Vol. LXX, 1987, Series A.

Nicolas Valticos: "Future prospects for international labour standards", in *International Labour Review*, Vol. 118, No. 6, 1979, pp. 679-697.

Chapter 4

Purpose and contents of international labour standards

Purpose

The Preamble to the ILO Constitution sets out three reasons for the establishment of the Organisation, which constitute the fundamental justification for international legislative action on labour questions. They are as follows:

(1) The fact that "universal and lasting peace can be established only if it is based upon social justice". This was a prime motive for those who framed the ILO Constitution as an integral part of the 1919 peace treaty. In this context it was logical to refer to "the peace and harmony of the world". Fifty years later the same reasoning led to the award of the Nobel Peace Prize to the ILO.

(2) The existence of conditions of labour involving "injustice, hardship and privation" and the need for their improvement. This motive is underlined in the Preamble by a reference to "sentiments of justice and humanity". It is reaffirmed in the passage of the Declaration of Philadelphia which affirms that "all human beings, irrespective of race, creed or sex, have the right to pursue both their material well-being and their spiritual development in conditions of freedom and dignity, of economic security and equal opportunity". The Preamble to the Constitution also sets out fields in which improvements in conditions of labour were "urgently required". All these are now covered by international labour standards.

(3) Fear of the social effects of international competition. The Preamble acknowledges that "the failure of any nation to adopt humane conditions of labour is an obstacle in the way of other nations which desire to improve the conditions in their own countries". The Declaration of Philadelphia recalls that "poverty anywhere constitutes a danger to prosperity anywhere". When the first Convention, the Hours of Work (Industry) Convention, was being discussed in 1919 one of the arguments put forward in support of it was that international regulation would make possible the simultaneous acceptance of the 48-hour week

which individual countries might hesitate to accept on a purely national basis, for fear of damaging their export position.

Apart from these three main reasons a number of other factors explain why Conventions and Recommendations are needed. They may be summarised as follows:

(4) The need for regulation of situations in which an international element is involved, such as the international mobility of labour. Seafarers and migrant workers are obvious examples.

(5) The technological complexity of much modern industry, which requires the pooling of national experience and the co-operation of high-level scientists and technicians for the elaboration of effective standards. A good example is Convention No. 115, concerning the protection of workers against ionising radiation.

(6) The value to many countries of a model on which to base their industrial legislation, after being suitably adapted, of course, to national circumstances. Many developing countries have attained independence with little to build on in the way of labour standards, and most tend to be short of the specialist staff required to draft legislation.

(7) What has been called the "safety stop" argument. When a country ratifies an ILO Convention it is, in effect, giving its pledge to an international treaty. By the same token, if a government takes measures inconsistent with its terms it will be violating an international treaty. Backsliding is therefore much more difficult than if no international obligations existed; hence ratification gives labour laws a degree of stability that is not necessarily conferred by purely national legislation. This argument answers the question "Why should we ratify an international convention when we already have comparable legislation in our statute book?"

Contents

The term "the International Labour Code" is often used to denote the whole body of Conventions and Recommendations adopted over the years by the International Labour Conference. By mid-1997 that Code consisted of 181 Conventions and 188 Recommendations covering an enormous range of important subjects in the labour and social fields (a classified guide, listing these instruments under 13 major headings, is among the appendices to this manual).

Strictly speaking, the International Labour Code is composed only of Conventions and Recommendations. However, in addition to these standards there are a series of resolutions, conclusions or codes of practice (some of them are listed in the bibliography appended to this manual) adopted either by the Conference or by technical meetings such as meetings of Industrial Committees or meetings of experts. These texts do not have the same character as Conventions or Recommendations. For example, a Conference resolution on civil liberties and trade union rights or a code of practice on safety and health in shipbuilding can never give rise to any formal reporting obligations. Nevertheless, these texts constitute a vast body of social policy guide-lines and form an important supplement to the International Labour Code in the narrow sense.

It would carry us too far to try to analyse the contents of all or even most of the existing international labour standards; nor is that the purpose of this manual, which is rather to enable the reader to understand how the ILO's standard-setting machinery and procedures work and what are the roles and responsibilities of workers and their organisations in the standard-setting process. Nevertheless, let us take a look at the contents of the principal Conventions and Recommendations adopted since 1919.

Basic human rights

The ILO has always attached particular importance to certain basic human rights which constitute an essential element in all action designed to improve the conditions of workers. These are dealt with in the Conventions and Recommendations on freedom of association, freedom from forced labour and freedom from discrimination.[1]

The workers have called for a campaign in favour of a world charter aiming primarily at universal ratification of the core human rights Conventions of the ILO, namely:

Core human rights Conventions

Forced Labour Convention, 1930 (No. 29)

Freedom of Association and Protection of the Right to Organise Convention, 1948 (No. 87)

Right to Organise and Collective Bargaining Convention, 1949 (No. 98)

Equal Remuneration Convention, 1951 (No. 100)

Abolition of Forced Labour Convention, 1957 (No. 105)

Discrimination (Employment and Occupation) Convention, 1958 (No. 111)

Minimum Age Convention, 1973 (No. 138)

In February 1995, the Committee on Legal Issues and International Labour Standards invited the Governing Body to ask the ILO to launch a campaign to promote the ILO's fundamental human rights Conventions. The Director-General has sent several letters and made other approaches to member States, and the rate of ratification of these Conventions has improved markedly.

Freedom of association. The basic ILO Conventions on freedom of association are the Freedom of Association and Protection of the Right to Organise Convention, 1948 (No. 87), and the Right to Organise and Collective Bargaining Convention, 1949 (No. 98).

Convention No. 87 is one of the most important of all ILO Conventions, and the one most valued by workers everywhere. It provides that workers and employers, without distinction whatsoever, shall have the right to establish and join organisations of their own choosing without previous authorisation. It also provides for guarantees permitting those organisations, and any federations they may establish, to carry on their activities without interference from the public authorities. Member States ratifying the Convention are to take all necessary and appropriate measures to ensure that workers and employers may exercise freely the right to organise.

Convention No. 98 is designed to protect workers against acts of anti-union discrimination, to safeguard workers' and employers' organisations from mutual interference, and to promote voluntary negotiation between management and labour.

Further standards, which reinforce these two basic Conventions, have been adopted in recent years. These include the Workers' Representatives Convention (No. 135), and Recommendation (No. 143), both of 1971, which aim at ensuring that workers' representatives in enterprises are effectively protected against any prejudicial act based on their status or activities as workers' representatives or on their union activities and provide that facilities shall be afforded in the enterprise to enable those representatives to carry out their functions promptly and efficiently; they also include the Rural Workers' Organisations Convention (No. 141), and Recommendation (No. 149), of 1975, which lay down the principle that all categories of rural workers are entitled to establish and join organisations of their own choosing, and provide that measures must be taken to facilitate the establishment and growth of strong and independent organisations of this kind; and the Labour Relations (Public Service) Convention (No. 151), and Recommendation (No. 159), of 1978, which are designed to safeguard and promote the right to organise and the development of suitable machinery for determining conditions of employment and settling disputes in the public service (see also Chapter 8 below).

Freedom from forced labour. The question of freedom of labour has been dealt with in two ILO Conventions. The Forced Labour Convention, 1930 (No. 29), provides for the progressive abolition of forced labour in all its forms and, pending this abolition, its use only for public purposes and as an exceptional measure, subject to the conditions and guarantees set out in detail in the various Articles of the Convention.

Convention No. 29 approached the problem of forced labour mainly from the point of view of practices then current in colonial territories. At a later stage, however, international attention became drawn to the widespread existence of forced labour also as a means of political coercion or for economic purposes. The abolition of such systems of forced labour was one of the main objectives of the Abolition of Forced Labour Convention (No. 105) adopted by the International Labour Conference in 1957. This Convention calls for the immediate and complete abolition of forced or compulsory labour for political purposes, as a method of mobilising and using labour for purposes of economic development, as a means of labour discipline, as a punishment for having participated in strikes and as a means of racial, social, national or religious discrimination.

Discrimination and equality of opportunity and treatment. The adoption in 1951 of a Convention (No. 100) concerning equal remuneration for men and women workers for work of equal value proved to be one of the landmarks in the ILO's standard-setting activities, and led to action in a great many countries. It provides that ratifying States must promote and, in so far as is consistent with the methods in operation for determining wages, ensure the application of this principle of equality, and that this should be done by means of legislation, collective agreements or wage-fixing machinery. Stress is laid, in this connection, on the importance of promoting the objective appraisal of jobs on the basis of the work to be performed.

In 1958 the International Labour Conference adopted both a Convention (No. 111) and a Recommendation (No. 111) on discrimination in employment and occupation. Both instruments refer to grounds of discrimination as diverse as race, sex or political opinion, for example. They cover discriminatory laws or acts in very general terms such as "any discrimination, exclusion or preference ... which has the effect of nullifying or impairing equality of treatment", and which can be the result not only of legislation but also of existing factual situations or practices. They reach into all sectors of employment and occupation, both public and private, and extend to vocational training and access to employment and to particular occupations, as well as to conditions of employment in general. The methods proposed in these texts to combat discrimination range from direct intervention through legislation to educational activities, and from action by the State to action by employers' and workers' organisations; individual countries are left a fairly wide margin of discretion.

The continuing increase in the number of women working outside their homes and having difficulty in reconciling their dual family and work responsibilities had led to the adoption in 1965 of a Recommendation (No. 123) on women with family responsibilities. This Recommendation was superseded in 1981 by Convention No. 156 and Recommendation No. 165. These instruments, which cover all workers with family responsibilities, provide for the adoption of policies and measures in such fields as vocational guidance and training, hours of work, leave, child-care facilities and social security to enable the workers concerned to exercise their right to engage in employment without being subject to discrimination and without conflict between their family and work responsibilities.

Employment

Employment policy. The first concern of a worker will always be simply to have a job, and certain ILO Recommendations adopted just before and after the Second World War already reflect the view that this can best be achieved through an active employment policy. However, it was not until 1964 that the Conference adopted the Employment Policy Convention (No. 122) and Recommendation (No. 122), the latter being expanded in 1984 by the Employment Policy (Supplementary Provisions) Recommendation (No. 169). The Convention provides that each ratifying State must pursue as a major goal an active policy designed to promote full, productive and freely chosen employment. This is to be done in consultation with the representatives of workers and employers, by methods appropriate to national conditions, and with due account taken of the level of economic development in the country concerned. More detailed guide-lines as to the measures to be taken are contained in the accompanying Recommendation.

In 1988 the Conference adopted the Employment Promotion and Protection against Unemployment Convention (No. 168) and Recommendation (No. 176). The Convention requires each ratifying State to take appropriate steps to co-ordinate its system of protection against unemployment and its employment policy. The system of protection against unemployment should be such as to contribute to the promotion of full, productive and freely chosen employment. The governments are obliged to implement the provisions of the Convention in consultation and co-operation with the organisations of employers and workers. The persons protected by the Convention must not comprise less than 85 per cent of all employees, including public employees and apprentices.

Employment services and agencies. Convention No. 2, requiring the establishment of a system of free public employment agencies, dates back to 1919. This obligation to maintain a free public employment service is set out in more concrete terms in Convention No. 88, of 1948, and the corresponding Recommendation (No. 83). The Convention specifies that the essential duty of the service is to ensure the best possible organisation of the employment market as an integral part of the national programme for the achievement and maintenance of full employment. It contains detailed provisions on the organisation of the service, and calls for co-operation with representatives of workers and employers.

The ILO has also concerned itself over the years with abuses arising out of fee-charging employment agencies. The latest instrument on the subject is the Private Employment Agencies Convention, 1997 (No. 181).

Vocational training and guidance. The importance of vocational and technical education, initially emphasised in the ILO Constitution in 1919, has been reflected in a series of standards adopted over the years. The latest and most important of these is the Human Resources Development Convention, 1975 (No. 142). This requires all ratifying States to adopt and develop comprehensive programmes of vocational guidance and training, taking account of employment needs and the level of economic objectives. The programmes are to enable all persons without discrimination to develop and use their capabilities for work. The means by which the policies and programmes in question should be developed and implemented are indicated in detail in the Convention and in the supplementary Recommendation (No. 150).

Rehabilitation and employment of disabled persons. The importance of care of disabled persons was first discussed by the Conference in 1955 when Recommendation No. 99 was adopted. It recommends the establishment of vocational rehabilitation services available to all disabled persons, irrespective of the origin and nature of their disability or of their age; further, it introduces the principles and methods of vocational guidance, vocational training and placement of such persons. Convention No. 159, of 1983, supplemented by Recommendation No. 168, requires the ratifying State to formulate, implement and periodically review a national policy on vocational rehabilitation and employment of disabled persons, in accordance with national conditions, practice and possibilities. It sets up the principles of such policies and determines action to be taken at the national level to this effect.

Employment security. The important question of the protection of workers in case of termination of employment at the initiative of the employer is dealt with in Convention No. 158 and Recommendation No. 166, of 1982 (see also below under "Industrial relations").

Social policy

Most ILO instruments deal with a well-defined, specific subject. However, in 1947 the Conference adopted a Convention (No. 82) concerning social policy in non-metropolitan territories, subsequently revised by a new Convention (No. 117) concerning basic aims and standards of social policy. These Conventions not only lay down the principle that all policies are to be directed primarily to the well-being and development of the population, but also contain a number of basic standards regarding, for example, wage rates, the protection of wages, freedom from discrimination, the minimum age of admission to employment, and education. Another text of a general nature was adopted in 1966: Recommendation No. 127, concerning the role of all categories of co-operatives in the economic and social development of developing countries. This text indicates the objectives of the policy to be followed in regard to co-operatives and the methods of implementing this policy.

Labour administration

The existence of a competent and efficient department of labour in each country is essential if the proper application of labour legislation and social policies is to be guaranteed. In 1978 the Conference adopted a Convention and a Recommendation on the role, functions and organisation of such departments.

Labour inspection. Certain aspects of labour inspection were covered in some of the earliest ILO Recommendations, going back to 1919. However, the basic Convention (No. 81) and Recommendation (No. 81) on labour inspection in industry and commerce were adopted in 1947, and were followed in 1969 by another Convention (No. 129) and Recommendation (No. 133) on agriculture. These standards contain a series of requirements concerning the system of labour inspection which must be maintained, including provisions on its functions and organisation, and on the status, training, duties and rights of inspectors.

In 1995, the International Labour Conference adopted a Protocol which extends the application of Convention No. 81 to the non-commercial services sector. Ratifying States may exclude wholly or partly from its scope the following categories: essential national (federal) government administration, the armed services, police and public security services, and prison staff and prisoners when performing work. They may also restrict inspection during firefighting, rescue or other emergency operations.

Statistics. The obligation to compile statistics on wages and hours of work is laid down in Convention No. 63, of 1938. Convention No. 160

and Recommendation No. 170, both of 1985, enlarge on the various aspects of the obligation to regularly collect, compile and publish basic labour statistics. In designing or revising the concepts, definitions and methodology to this purpose, the member States ratifying the Convention are required to take into consideration the latest standards and guide-lines established under the auspices of the ILO.

Tripartite consultation. The fact that the ILO is a tripartite organisation, with participation of governments, employers and workers, should be reflected in the standards adopted by the Conference. Most of these provide for consultation with employers' and workers' organisations or representatives as regards the measures to be taken and their effective application. In 1976 the Conference also adopted two special texts which may have far-reaching consequences; these are Convention No. 144 and Recommendation No. 152. The first provides for an obligation to operate procedures designed essentially to secure tripartite consultation with a view to promoting the application of ILO Conventions and Recommendations. The second, that is the Recommendation, provides for such consultations not only as regards ILO standards but also as regards national action relating to the activities of the ILO. Repeated references are made to these standards elsewhere in this manual.

Industrial relations

The basic standards governing industrial relations, that is the freedom of association Conventions, have been mentioned above. In addition, however, a series of other instruments have been adopted over the years on various aspects of relations between employers and workers.

Thus, in 1951 the Conference adopted a Recommendation (No. 91) dealing with collective bargaining machinery, and the effects of collective agreements, their extension and interpretation, and also the supervision of their application. The principles that should govern voluntary conciliation and arbitration are briefly set out in another Recommendation (No. 92) of 1951. A Recommendation (No. 94) adopted in 1952 provides that steps should be taken, by means of legislation or otherwise, to promote consultation and co-operation between employers and workers at the level of enterprises on matters of mutual concern not dealt with by other machinery. The need for measures promoting such consultation and co-operation at higher levels – that is at the industrial and national levels – is set out in Recommendation No. 113, of 1960. This text indicates that the aim of this consultation should be, on the one hand, to help arrive at agreed solutions between employers' and workers' organisations and, on the other hand, to ensure that those organisations are consulted by the public authorities regarding the preparation and implementation of social legislation, the establishment and functioning of national bodies, and plans of economic and social development. In 1981, the Collective Bargaining Convention (No. 154), and Recommendation (No. 163), were adopted in order to encourage and promote the development of collective bargaining by means adapted to national conditions.

A particularly important text was adopted in 1963: the Recommendation (No. 119) concerning the termination of employment at the initiative of the employer, which has had considerable influence on the legislation of many countries. The Recommendation lays down the principle that termination should not take place unless there is a valid reason connected with the capacity or conduct of the worker or based on the operational requirements of the enterprise or establishment. It also enumerates reasons which should not be considered as valid (such as union membership or discrimination on various other grounds) and describes various measures to be taken in order to protect workers against unjustified dismissal. New standards on the subject, embodying these basic principles as well as improvements in other provisions of the Recommendation, which reflect recent developments in the law and practice in many countries, are set forth in Convention No. 158 and Recommendation No. 166 adopted by the 68th Session of the Conference in 1982.

Mention should also be made of two other important Recommendations, adopted in 1967. The first of these (No. 129) concerns communications between management and workers in enterprises; it indicates certain general considerations which should be borne in mind and also describes the elements of the communication policy which should be applied in enterprises. The second Recommendation (No. 130) is concerned with the examination of grievances within enterprises with a view to their settlement. It contains provisions on the right of workers to submit grievances, on the procedures to be followed within enterprises in order to settle such grievances, and also on the measures to be taken in regard to unsettled grievances (see also Chapter 8 below).

Conditions of work

Wages. The obligation to provide machinery to lay down minimum wages was first established in a Convention (No. 26) and a Recommendation (No. 30) in 1928. As these apply only to manufacturing – including homeworking trades – and commerce, the International Labour Conference adopted in 1951 a further Convention (No. 99) and Recommendation (No. 89) applying to agriculture. These texts provide for an obligation to create or maintain machinery for the establishment of minimum wage rates, in co-operation with representatives of the employers and workers concerned. They also prescribe a system of supervision and penalties. The latest standards on the question are set out in Convention No. 131 and Recommendation No. 135, of 1970, which pay special regard to the needs of developing countries. These texts provide for an obligation to establish a system of minimum wages covering all workers whose terms of employment are such that coverage would be appropriate, and for the creation of appropriate machinery. In addition they indicate, for example, the factors to be taken into consideration in determining the wage levels, and provide for the periodic adjustment of those levels.

Requirements regarding the protection of wages are to be found in a number of Conventions and Recommendations, the main one being the Protection of Wages Convention, 1949 (No. 95), and the supplementary Recommendation (No. 85). This Convention, which is of general application, is designed to protect workers against practices that might make them unduly dependent on the employer, and also to ensure that wages are paid in full and without delay. In this context, we should also mention the Protection of Workers' Claims (Employer's Insolvency) Convention, 1992 (No. 173) and Recommendation (No. 180).

Hours of work, night work and holidays. The very first Convention of the ILO, No. 1, of 1919, fixes maximum working hours in industry at eight per day and 48 per week. Some years later another Convention was adopted (No. 30, of 1930) providing for the same levels in commerce and offices. Both these Conventions authorise a limited number of exceptions as regards scope, and permit longer hours in certain specific cases, subject to strict conditions. The principle of the 40-hour week was set out in Convention No. 47, of 1935, and more recently, in 1962, a Recommendation (No. 116) was adopted which provides that each State should formulate and pursue a policy designed to introduce a

40-hour week without any reduction of wages. This text also contains provisions on the calculation of working hours, permissible exceptions, overtime, supervision and sanctions. A Convention (No. 153) and Recommendation (No. 161), of 1979, deal with hours of work and rest periods for road transport workers.

Standards on night work concerning the protection of women, children and young people are referred to below. The Night Work Convention (No. 171) and Recommendation (No. 178) were adopted in 1990 to cover all employed persons except in agriculture, stock raising, fishing, maritime transport and inland navigation, and aim to protect the safety and health of night workers, to assist them to meet their family and social responsibilities, provide opportunities for occupational advancement, and compensate them appropriately.

Weekly rest is prescribed in Convention No. 44, of 1921, as regards industry and in Convention No. 106, of 1957, as regards commerce and offices. A certain amount of flexibility is allowed in both of these texts.

The first Convention on holidays with pay, No. 52, of 1936, provides merely for one week's leave after one year's continuous service for workers in industry, commerce and offices, but was adopted at a time when very few countries had accepted the idea of such holidays. As regards agricultural workers, their holiday rights are provided for in a later Convention (No. 101, of 1952). Convention No. 52 had a remarkable influence on national law and practice, and the rapid evolution in views on annual holidays is reflected in the terms of a new Convention (No. 132) which was adopted in 1970. Convention No. 132 applies to all employed workers (except seafarers), and provides for an annual holiday which may not be less than three weeks, or a proportionate holiday when the length of service is less than a year. Of particular importance for workers is another recent Convention (No. 140, of 1974) which marks a new concept of paid leave: it recognises both the need for continuing education and training and the fact that these needs must be met, at least in part, by means of paid educational leave (that is, leave granted during working hours, with adequate financial entitlements) for the purpose of training at all levels, of general education and of trade union education. The Convention is supplemented by Recommendation No. 148.

The Part-Time Work Convention, 1994 (No. 175), and Recommendation (No. 182) aim to ensure that part-time workers receive the same or equivalent protection or conditions comparable to full-time workers and that additional employment opportunities are facilitated. The Home Work Convention (No. 177) and Recommendation (No. 184), adopted in 1996, indicate measures to be taken to improve the situation of homeworkers.

Occupational safety and health. Questions relating to the health and safety of workers have always been to the forefront of the ILO's concerns: they are featured in its Constitution and were in fact the subject of four Recommendations adopted in 1919, at the First Session of the Conference. Altogether more than 30 Conventions and even more Recommendations dealing with the problems of health, safety and welfare of workers have been adopted.

Among the more general texts, we find Recommendation No. 31, of 1929, regarding the prevention of industrial accidents and Recommendation No. 97, of 1953, on the protection of the health of workers in their workplace.

In 1981 the Conference adopted a Convention (No. 155) and Recommendation (No. 164) concerning the principles involved and the action needed (both at the national and the plant levels) to ensure greater occupational safety and health in the working environment. Following an initial Recommendation (No. 112) in 1959, the Conference adopted Convention No. 161 and Recommendation No. 171 on occupational health services in or near places of employment, in 1985. There are also a number of standards that are designed to protect workers against specific risks. Some relate to risks due to toxic substances such as white lead (Convention No. 13, of 1921) or benzene (Convention No. 136, of 1971), to carcinogenic substances and agents (Convention No. 139, of 1974), to exposure to ionising radiation (Convention No. 115, of 1960) or to asbestos (Convention No. 162, of 1986). In 1977 the Conference adopted a Convention (No. 148) and Recommendation (No. 156) with the aim of protecting workers in all branches of activity against occupational hazards in the working environment due to air pollution, noise and vibration. These two texts give details of the preventive and protective measures to be taken and the means of ensuring their application. The Conference has also adopted a Convention (No. 119, of 1963) prohibiting, the sale, hire and use of inadequately guarded machinery and laying down detailed prescriptions on the subject, and another (No. 127, of 1967) dealing with the maximum permissible weight which may be carried by one worker. Applicable to all branches of economic activity in which chemicals are used, the Chemicals Convention, 1990 (No. 170), calls on member States to formulate, implement and review a coherent policy on safety in the use of chemicals at work. The competent authority should be able, if appropriate, to prohibit or restrict the use of certain hazardous chemicals.

The various forms of special protection needed in given branches of activity are also covered by certain ILO Conventions and Recommendations, including Convention No. 72, of 1937, and the supplementary Recommendation (No. 53), which contain detailed provisions concerning safety in the building industry; Convention No. 167, of 1988, and the supplementary Recommendation (No. 175), concerning safety measures in all construction activities and applicable to any person engaged in construction; Convention No. 120, of 1964, and its accompanying Recommendation (also No. 120), which lay down the general principles and describe the measures to be taken as regards hygiene in commerce and offices; and a series of Conventions and Recommendations designed to protect dockworkers against accidents (Conventions Nos. 27 and 28, of 1929, and No. 32, of 1932, and Recommendations Nos. 33 and 34, of 1929, and No. 40, of 1932, and Convention No. 152 and Recommendation No. 160, of 1979).

Still in this area, the Prevention of Major Industrial Accidents Convention, 1993 (No. 174), lays down the responsibilities of employers, the competent authorities and exporting States, giving lists of dispositions to be taken with regard to identification, notification, reporting, emergency preparedness and so on, as well as enumerating the rights and duties of workers and their representatives. The Recommendation (No. 181) essentially arranges for an international exchange of information on accidents and hazards.

Finally, the Safety and Health in Mines Convention, 1995 (No. 176), and Recommendation (No. 183), require member States to formulate, carry out and periodically review policy and legislation on supervision, inspection, reporting, and investigation, as well as to compile and publish statistics on accidents, diseases and dangerous occurrences. The Convention requires employers to evaluate and eliminate or reduce risks to safety and health, to prepare emergency plans, to inform workers fully about the risks, and provide appropriate equipment, protection, training and health care; it also outlines the rights and duties of workers and their representatives.

Social services, housing and leisure. No ILO Conventions have so far dealt exclusively with social services, housing and leisure but those questions are covered in detail in certain Recommendations: No. 102, of 1956, which lays down the standards to be observed in enterprises as regards feeding, rest and recreation facilities and as regards transport; No. 115, of 1961, on workers' housing, which contains provisions on the national housing policy to be followed, responsibilities for applying it and financing, as well as suggested methods of application; and also an early text, No. 21, of 1924, which both seeks to preserve the leisure of workers by discouraging them from having recourse to additional paid work and suggests various measures for improving the utilisation of spare time.

Social security

Many ILO Conventions and Recommendations are concerned with the promotion of social security for workers and their families. Those adopted before the Second World War deal with particular risks or contingencies, whereas the more recent standards cover all or several branches of social security. The basic text is Convention No. 102, of 1952, which lays down minimum standards of social security, and which covers nine branches (medical care, sickness, unemployment, old age, employment injury, family, maternity, invalidity and survivors' benefits). Each ratifying State must undertake to observe the standards prescribed as regards at least three of these branches for specified categories of workers or sectors of the population, and can of course subsequently accept obligations as regards other branches also. This Convention marks a turning-point in social security standards by introducing the idea of a general level of social security that can be attained everywhere, since the system can be adapted to the economic and social conditions prevailing in each country, whatever the degree of its development.

The standards laid down since 1919 in the many Conventions and Recommendations on the various branches of social security are briefly as follows:

Medical care. Two ILO Conventions adopted in 1927 (Nos. 24 and 25) provide for compulsory sickness insurance systems in industry and agriculture respectively. Benefits include medical treatment and the supply of medicines and appliances, free of charge. Convention No. 102 describes in detail the medical care of a preventive or curative nature to be guaranteed, and extends the benefits to include hospitalisation.

Sickness benefit. The above-mentioned Conventions of 1927 (Nos. 24 and 25) also provide for the payment of cash benefits in case of sickness. Convention No. 102, of 1952, goes further in that it fixes the minimum level of benefits in its general provisions on periodical payments. The latest Convention on the subject (No. 130, of 1969) fixes a higher level of benefits and has a wider scope, and the supplementary Recommendation (No. 134) provides that the sickness benefit legislation should be applicable to all economically active members of the population.

Maternity benefit. The right to maternity benefit is prescribed in two Conventions on maternity protection, the first of which (No. 3, of 1919) is applicable only to women employed in industry and commerce whereas the second (No. 103, of 1952) also applies to workers in agriculture and other non-industrial occupations. Both texts provide for cash benefits during the period of maternity leave and for medical care, to be granted through a compulsory social insurance system or by means of public funds. Under Convention No. 103 the benefit must be not less than two-thirds of the woman's previous earnings when it is provided under an insurance scheme and is based on earnings. Convention No. 102 also contains a part on maternity benefit. A proposal to revise Conventions Nos. 3 and 103 will be submitted to the 87th Session of the International Labour Conference in 1999.

Invalidity benefit. The first ILO Conventions on the subject of invalidity benefit were adopted in 1933, and they applied to industry (No. 37) and agriculture (No. 38). They provide for the payment of an invalidity pension, under compulsory invalidity insurance schemes, to insured persons who become generally incapacitated for work. Convention No. 102 provides for such benefits also. These standards were revised by Convention No. 128, of 1967, which provides for a minimum level of benefits higher than that required under Convention No. 102 and also lays down obligations regarding rehabilitation services and the placement of disabled persons. The corresponding Recommendation (No. 131, also of 1967) provides for the extension of the relevant legislation to all economically active persons.

Old-age benefit. In 1933 two Conventions were adopted to provide for compulsory insurance schemes under which old-age pensions would be paid at a prescribed age, not to exceed 65, to insured persons in industry (Convention No. 35) and in agriculture (Convention No. 36). Convention No. 102 provides that old-age pensions must not be lower than a prescribed level. Convention No. 128, of 1967, revises these earlier standards, and provides for old-age pensions on more favourable terms than were previously laid down.

Survivors' benefit. The obligation to provide for compulsory widows' and orphans' insurance was also first established in 1933, in Convention No. 39 as regards industry and in Convention No. 40 as regards agriculture. Convention No. 102, unlike the earlier texts, fixes the minimum rate of survivors' benefits payable under such schemes, and Convention No. 28 – which revises the previous Conventions on the subject – provides for a minimum rate of benefit which is superior to that fixed by Convention No. 102.

Employment injury benefit. Convention No. 12, adopted in 1921, merely provides that agricultural workers are to be covered by any existing legislation on workmen's compensation. Convention No. 17, of 1925, on the other hand, lays down basic rules on the subject, specifying that compensation – normally in the form of periodic payments – must be paid to workers or their dependants where permanent incapacity or death results from an industrial accident. Another text adopted in 1925, Convention No. 18 (subsequently revised by Convention No. 42, of 1934), provides for the payment of compensation for occupational diseases in accordance with the general principles of the legislation relating to compensation for industrial accidents. Convention No. 102 also contains a part requiring the grant of employment injury benefit in the case of an accident or a prescribed disease arising out of employment, to take the form of medical care and periodical payments. Twelve years after the adoption of Convention No. 102, these standards were revised by Convention No. 121, of 1964, which ensures more extensive protection than was specified in Convention No. 102 – wider scope as regards persons covered, improved medical care and related services and provisions regarding the minimum rate of the periodical payments.

Unemployment benefit. It was only in 1934 that a Convention (No. 44) was adopted which required ratifying States to set up a system for the payment of benefits – as distinct from assistance – to the involuntarily unemployed. Detailed provisions regarding unemployment benefit were also laid down in Convention No. 102, which specifies how the periodical payments are to be calculated. However, in 1988 the Conference adopted Convention No. 168 and Recommendation No. 176 (already mentioned above, in the section on employment policy) which provide for benefits in cases of full unemployment, partial unemployment and temporary suspension of work.

Family benefit. Convention No. 102 provides for the granting of benefits for the maintenance of children. These benefits may take the form of periodical payments or allowances in kind, or a combination of the two.

Social security and migrants. Most social insurance or social security Conventions provide specially for equality of treatment either as regards all foreign workers or at least as regards nationals of other States having ratified the Convention in question. In the case of accident compensation, a special Convention (No. 19) was adopted in 1925 providing that ratifying countries must grant to the nationals of other countries bound by the Convention the same rights as to their own nationals as regards workmen's compensation for accidents, and that no condition as to residence may be imposed. A more recent Convention, No. 118, of 1962, provides for equality of treatment to be granted to workers of other ratifying countries, as regards all nine branches of social security, although the obligations of the Convention may be accepted as regards only one of those branches.

The question of the maintenance of the acquired rights of migrant workers, or of rights which they are in course of acquiring, gives rise to special problems because of the varying principles governing national legislation. The desire to find a solution to these problems led to the adoption of Convention No. 48, of 1935, which provides for the establishment of an international scheme for the maintenance of rights under invalidity, old-age and widows' and orphans' insurance. In 1982 the Conference adopted Convention No. 157, revising Convention No. 48 and supplementing Convention No. 118, with regard to the maintenance of rights under all branches of social security. In addition, in 1983 the Conference adopted Recommendation No. 167, with an appended model agreement, to facilitate the conclusion between member States of bilateral or multilateral agreements with a view to safeguarding the detailed maintenance of rights.

Employment of women

The earlier ILO standards on the employment of women aimed essentially at protecting them against abuses in their conditions of work, particularly in the case of maternity, whereas the more recent standards (including Convention No. 100, on equal remuneration, and Convention No. 111, on discrimination, which are mentioned above) are designed to secure for women workers the same rights and treatment as those enjoyed by men.

Maternity protection. As we have already seen above, the maternity protection Conventions (Nos. 3 and 103, of 1919 and 1952 respectively) provide for social security benefits and medical care. In addition, however, they establish the right to maternity leave of not less than 12 weeks. Thus Convention No. 3, which applies only to industry, provides that six weeks of leave must be taken before childbirth and six weeks after. Convention No. 103, which is of general application, is more flexible and merely specifies that at least six of the 12 weeks' leave must be taken after childbirth. Under both Conventions the post-confinement leave is obligatory and must be extended in certain cases. These instruments also provide that an employer may not dismiss a woman while she is on maternity leave, or give her notice of dismissal at such a time that it would expire while she is on leave.

Night work. Three Conventions prohibiting the employment of women at night have been adopted: No. 4, of 1919, was revised by No. 41, of 1934, and again by No. 89, of 1948. This last Convention, which is more flexible than the earlier ones, prohibits night work by women in industrial undertakings during a period of 11 consecutive hours.[2]

Underground work. A Convention (No. 45) adopted in 1935 prohibits the employment of women on underground work in mines of all kinds.

Employment of children and young persons

The first Convention on child labour, the Minimum Age (Industry) Convention, 1919 (No. 5), was adopted in 1919, the year of the ILO's foundation. It prohibits the work of children under the age of 14 in industrial establishments. Subsequently, nine sectoral Conventions on the minimum age of admission to employment were adopted, applying to industry, agriculture, trimmers and stokers, maritime work, non-industrial employment, fishing and underground work. Other ILO standards contain provisions setting minimum ages for various activities.

The most recent and comprehensive ILO instruments on child labour are the Minimum Age Convention, 1973 (No. 138), and Recommendation (No. 146). Convention No. 138 is a consolidation of principles that had been gradually established in various earlier instruments and applies to all sectors of economic activity, whether or not the children are employed for wages. It obliges ratifying States to pursue a national policy designed to ensure the effective abolition of child labour and to raise progressively the minimum age for admission to employment to a level consistent with the fullest physical and mental development of young people.

The Convention provides that the minimum age should not be less than the age for completing compulsory schooling and in no event less than age 15. However, developing countries can initially fix the minimum age at 14. Employers' and workers' organizations must be consulted before making use of this flexibility clause, as in many other cases where national determination is required under this Convention.

It also sets a higher minimum age of 18 for hazardous work, "which by its nature or the circumstances in which it is carried out is likely to jeopardize the health, safety or morals of young persons". The list of such hazardous work must be established after consultation with the employers' and workers' organisations concerned.

Although the Convention is, in principle, to be applied to all sectors of activity, whether or not children are employed for wages, flexibility is built in to allow exceptions and progressive implementation. For example, light work, provided that it is not hazardous and would not hinder education, may be permitted from age 13 (12 in developing countries where the minimum age is fixed at 14 instead of 15).[3] There is no exception for developing countries, however, concerning hazardous work (age 18), which is consistent with the principle that the level of development is no excuse for allowing children to be exposed to work likely to jeopardize their health, safety and morals.

In 1996 the Governing Body decided to include child labour on the agenda for the 1998 and 1999 sessions of the International Labour Conference, with a view to adopting new standards prohibiting child labour in its extreme forms. The new instruments would set priority targets in the fight against child labour under the existing standards, and focus on its worst forms, including hazardous work, forced or bonded labour, prostitution and production of pornography, and on measures to eradicate or combat these forms.

Night work. Convention No. 6, of 1919, provides that young persons under 18 years of age may not be employed in industrial undertakings at night. This prohibition applies to a period of 11 consecutive hours, including the period between 10 p.m. and 5 a.m. This text was revised by Convention No. 90, of 1948, which increased the period to 12 consecutive hours and provided for measures of application but otherwise allows for greater flexibility. As regards non-industrial employment, Convention No. 79, of 1946, prohibits night work for minimum periods of 12 or 14 hours, according to specified circumstances.

Medical examination. Two Conventions adopted in 1946 provide that children and young persons under 18 years of age are not to be admitted to employment unless they have been found fit for the work in question by a thorough medical examination. The first of these Conventions (No. 77) concerns work in industry and the second (No. 78) concerns non-industrial occupations. These texts also provide for continuing medical examinations up to specified ages. Similar protective measures, but in conjunction with higher age limits, are provided for in Convention No. 124, of 1965, regarding underground work.

Underground work. Recommendation No. 125, of 1965, provides for conditions of employment of young persons underground in mines and quarries.

Older workers

A Recommendation (No. 162) adopted in 1980 advocates the adoption of a policy to prevent any discrimination against older workers, and of measures to enable them to continue in employment under satisfactory conditions and to prepare themselves to retire on a voluntary basis, as far as possible.

Migrant workers

The ILO has for long been concerned with the special problems of migrant workers in general. The first text on the subject is Convention No. 97, of 1949, which contains a series of provisions designed on the one hand to assist migrants for employment and on the other hand to secure equality of treatment in various fields. In 1975 the ILO adopted Convention No. 143 and Recommendation No. 151, which contain further provisions aimed at eliminating abusive conditions and promoting equality of treatment and opportunity. In the first place Convention

No. 143 provides that governments must respect the basic human rights of all migrant workers. They must also prevent clandestine migration for employment and stop manpower trafficking activities. Secondly, governments must declare and pursue a policy to secure equality of treatment in respect of matters such as employment and occupation, social security, and trade union and cultural rights.

Indigenous workers and peoples

A certain number of standards have been adopted to protect indigenous workers against exploitation and coercion. The first of these is Convention No. 50, of 1936, which regulates certain systems of recruiting workers. Others include Conventions Nos. 65, of 1939, and 104, of 1955, which provide for the progressive or immediate abolition of penal sanctions for breaches of contracts, and Conventions Nos. 64, of 1939, and 86, of 1947, which aim at eliminating abuses in the conclusion of contracts of employment with indigenous workers.

These texts cover several aspects of work that were particularly relevant to conditions in dependent territories or colonies. Other Conventions adopted in 1947 were mainly designed to apply standards of a more general nature in such territories. These latter Conventions provide for the implementation of a sound social policy in the territories concerned (No. 82), for freedom of association (No. 84), for labour inspection (No. 85), and for the application of a series of international labour standards (No. 83).

In 1957, the Conference adopted Convention No. 107 and Recommendation No. 104, which apply to indigenous and tribal populations in independent countries and are aimed at protecting these peoples against abuses, securing their basic rights, and generally improving their living and working conditions. Finally, in 1989, Convention No. 169 was adopted, revising Convention No. 107 in the light of changes in the position of indigenous and tribal populations and of greater understanding of their position by governments, employers and workers alike.

Other special categories of workers

Seafarers

The special nature of conditions of work and of life of seafarers has led the Conference to adopt an extensive range of over 50 Conventions and Recommendations applying specifically to such workers or, in certain cases, to fishermen.[4]

General. Some of the standards adopted for seafarers are of a general nature. The most important of these is certainly Convention No. 147, of 1976, which aims at ensuring the observance in merchant ships of a wide range of standards including those laid down in many of the Conventions enumerated below. In particular, any ratifying country undertakes to have appropriate laws on safety, social security and conditions of work and life on board ship, and to verify their application by inspection or otherwise. Another important maritime Convention of a general nature is Convention No. 108, of 1958, which requires a government to issue a seafarer's identity document to each of its nationals who is a seafarer. The Merchant Shipping (Minimum Standards) Convention, 1976 (No. 147), has been supplemented by a Protocol of 1996.

Conditions for admission to employment. The minimum age for the admission of children to employment at sea was initially fixed at 14 years (Convention No. 7), but this was later raised to 15 years (Convention No. 58) or more (Convention No. 138). The obligation to undergo a medical examination prior to engagement was initially provided for young persons only (Convention No. 16), but was later extended to any person to be employed on board ship (Convention No. 73).

Certificates of competency. A number of ILO standards are designed to ensure that only properly qualified persons may be engaged for certain duties on board ship. Thus Convention No. 53, of 1936, contains provisions on the minimum requirement of professional competency for masters and officers, and Convention No. 74, of 1946, provides that able seamen must hold appropriate certificates of qualification. The obligation for a ship's cook to have a proper certificate is also prescribed, in Convention No. 69, of 1946.

Training, entry into employment and security of employment. The vocational training of seafarers is dealt with in detail in Recommendation No. 137, of 1970, and the special employment problems arising from technical developments on board ship are the subject of Recommendation No. 139, of the same year, which contains provisions on manpower planning, recruitment and placement (also dealt with in Convention No. 9, of 1920), training and retraining, and regularity of employment. The Recruitment and Placement of Seafarers Convention, 1996 (No. 179), and Recommendation No. 186 are the latest standards in this field. In addition, Convention No. 145 and Recommendation No. 154, both of 1976, provide that countries with a maritime industry must take steps to promote continuous or regular employment for qualified seafarers; and Convention No. 22, of 1926, specifies the manner in which articles of agreement are to be signed and terminated, and the particulars to be included in these documents.

General conditions of employment. Numerous texts on general conditions of employment have been adopted, the most important being Convention No. 109, of 1958, concerning wages, hours of work on board ship, and manning,[5] Conventions Nos. 91, of 1949, and 146, of 1976, which provide that seafarers shall be entitled to annual leave with pay of a specified minimum length, and Convention No. 23, of 1926, regarding the repatriation of seafarers who have been landed during the term of their engagement or on its expiration. The latter was revised by Convention No. 166 (supplemented by Recommendation No. 174), of 1987. Convention No. 180 and Recommendation No. 188 of 1996 concerning hours of work and manning are recent additions in this area. Recommendation No. 188 also covers wages.

Safety, health and welfare. Matters relating to the safety and health of seafarers are regulated in several ILO standards, including Convention No. 134 and Recommendation No. 142 (both of 1970) concerning the prevention of occupational accidents to seafarers, and two Recommendations (Nos. 105 and 106) of 1958 which contain provisions regarding medical advice by radio and the contents of medicine chests on board ship. Detailed requirements regarding crew accommodation are laid down in Conventions Nos. 92, of 1949, and 133, of 1970, and also in two Recommendations, Nos. 140 and 141, of 1970. The question of food and catering for crews is covered by Convention No. 68, of 1946, and provisions on seafarers' welfare in port and at sea are set out in Recommendations Nos. 48, of 1936, and 138, of 1970.

The 74th (Maritime) Session of the International Labour Conference adopted in 1987 a number of new instruments covering seafarers. Convention No. 163, supplemented by Recommendation No. 173, requires that each ratifying State ensure adequate welfare facilities and services at sea and in port for all seafarers, irrespective of nationality, race, colour, sex, religion, political opinion or social origin and irrespective of the State in which the ship on which they are employed is registered. Convention No. 164 provides for measures to ensure health protection and medical care for seafarers on board ship.

Social security. Already, in 1920, standards were adopted to provide for unemployment benefits for seafarers (Convention No. 8 and Recommendation No. 10) and in 1936 two further social security texts were adopted: Convention No. 55, which lays down the shipowners' liability in respect of sick and injured seafarers, and Convention No. 56, concerning sickness insurance for seafarers. Post-war standards relating to seafarers include Convention No. 70, of 1946, on social security for seafarers and Convention No. 71, of 1946, on seafarers' pensions.

In 1987, the 74th (Maritime) Session of the International Labour Conference adopted Convention No. 165 which revised both Convention No. 56, of 1936, on sickness insurance and Convention No. 70, of 1946, on social security for seafarers. According to the new Convention, the ratifying States are bound to comply with its provisions on minimum and superior standards in respect of at least three of the nine branches of social security (i.e. medical care, and benefits in case of sickness, unemployment, old age, employment injury, maternity, invalidity, as well as family and survivors' benefits). The Maritime Session of 1996 adopted the Labour Inspection (Seafarers) Convention (No. 178) and Recommendation (No. 185), the Recruitment and Placement of Seafarers Convention (No. 179) and Recommendation (No. 186), and the Seafarers' Hours of Work and the Manning of Ships Convention (No. 180) and its accompanying Recommendation (No. 187) which also covers wages. These revised earlier standards on the same subjects.

Fishermen

Since most of the Conventions concerning seafarers do not apply to fishermen, a series of texts have been adopted for this category of workers. They cover matters such as the minimum age for admission to employment as fishermen (Convention No. 112, of 1959), medical examinations (Convention No. 113, of 1959), articles of agreement (Convention No. 114, of 1959), competency certificates (Convention

No. 125, of 1966), accommodation of crews (Convention No. 126, of 1966) and vocational training (Recommendation No. 126, of 1966).

Agricultural workers

Many of the standards mentioned elsewhere in this chapter apply to agricultural workers, either because they are general in scope or because they provide for the application to agriculture of some given rights or protective measure (for example as regards freedom of association, social security or annual holidays). In addition to those standards, the Conference adopted in 1958 a Convention (No. 110) and Recommendation (No. 110) which provide for the application to plantation workers of a wide range of standards, including some relating to freedom of association, migrant workers, contracts of employment, wages, holidays, maternity protection, workmen's compensation, labour inspection, housing and medical care. Similarly, Recommendation No. 132, of 1968, indicates a series of measures to be taken in order to improve the conditions of work and of life of tenants, share-croppers and other categories of agricultural workers.

Dockworkers

The need for special measures regulating conditions of work of dockworkers is reflected in a number of standards, mentioned above under occupational health and safety. More recently, the ILO has adopted two important instruments on the subject, namely Convention No. 137 and Recommendation No. 145, both of 1973, on the social repercussions of the new methods of cargo handling in docks. These texts state that there should be a national policy to promote the regular employment of dockworkers, and indicate the means by which this policy must be implemented.

Nursing personnel

At its 1977 Session, the Conference adopted a Nursing Personnel Convention (No. 149), with a complementary Recommendation (No. 157), concerning the employment, training, career development, remuneration, hours of work and rest periods, health protection, and social security of nurses and their participation in the determination of conditions affecting their employment.

Notes

[1] The Conventions on basic human rights are not only among the most important of all ILO Conventions, but they are also among those which have been ratified by the largest number of countries. Thus, by 6 February 1998 the two freedom of association Conventions (Nos. 87 and 98) had been ratified by 120 and 134 countries respectively, the two Conventions on the abolition of forced labour (Nos. 29 and 105) had been ratified by 144 and 129 countries respectively, the Convention on freedom from discrimination in employment (No. 111) had been ratified by 127 countries, the Equal Remuneration Convention, 1951 (No. 100) by 132 countries, and the Minimum Age Convention, 1973 (No. 138) by 57 countries.

[2] It should be noted that while the type of protection provided for in these Conventions and in Convention No. 45 is regarded in many countries as being both necessary and beneficial, it is thought in some quarters that it is likely to be contrary to women's own interests: certainly the prohibition of work on certain shifts or in certain occupations may reduce the employment prospects of women and their chance of earning the same remuneration as men. A Protocol to the Night Work (Women) (Revised) Convention, 1948 (No. 89) was adopted in 1990, allowing variations in the duration of the night period and exemptions from the prohibition of night work, after consulting the most representative organisations of employers and workers. These variations and exemptions may be introduced in a specific branch of activity or occupation, or in one or more specific establishments.

[3] For more details in this regard see Chapter 3.

[4] This must not be taken to mean that other Conventions with a more general scope may not also be applicable to seafarers and fishermen.

[5] In spite of the fact that many countries have no interest or concern in matters relating to seafarers, the maritime Conventions have in some cases attracted a surprisingly high number of ratifications – often between 40 and 50. However, it is a fact that certain of those Conventions have been ratified by relatively few countries, and that they are often more useful as guide-lines than for the obligations they have created: in particular the three older ILO Conventions on wages, hours of work and manning are acknowledged to have been a major influence on seafarers' conditions of work, yet none of the three has received the minimum number of ratifications required for its entry into force. The standards adopted in 1996 (Convention No. 180 and Recommendation No. 188) are intended to be more widely observable.

Points for discussion

1. Describe the main categories of subjects dealt with in ILO instruments (Conventions and Recommendations).
2. What subjects are still missing in Conventions and Recommendations in your opinion?
3. What is your opinion about the fact that the protection afforded by Conventions and Recommendations is sometimes considered to be contrary to the interests of the persons concerned?
4. How many Conventions has your country ratified? Are the most important ones (particularly those dealing with basic human rights) among them?

Further reading

ILO: *International Labour Conventions and Recommendations 1919-1995* (with supplements), Geneva, 1996.

ILO: *Summaries of international labour standards*, second edition, Geneva, 1991.

ILO: *World Labour Report*, Vol. 2 (Geneva, 1985), Part 2: "International labour standards", pp. 55-85.

ILO: *Maritime labour Conventions and Recommendations*, fourth edition, Geneva, 1998.

Chapter 5

General application of standards: (I) Scope of the system

The ultimate aim of the standard-setting process is of course that the standards adopted should be accepted as widely as possible and then be put into effect. The ILO Constitution provides for a number of mutually complementary procedures for monitoring the effect given to Conventions and Recommendations adopted by the International Labour Conference. There is a procedure governing the submission of Conventions and Recommendations to the national authorities (article 19 of the Constitution). There is a procedure for reporting by member States on the position of their law and practice as regards the matters dealt with in Conventions which they have not ratified and in Recommendations (also article 19). A fundamentally important procedure relates to reporting by member States on the measures they have taken to apply effectively the Conventions which they have ratified (article 22). There is a procedure for the examination by the Governing Body of complaints (the formal term is in fact "representations") by workers' or employers' organisations that a member State is failing to apply a ratified Convention (articles 24 and 25). Finally, there is also a procedure for the examination by the Governing Body, and if the Governing Body so decides by a commission of inquiry appointed by it, of a complaint filed by a member State that another member State is failing to apply a Convention which both have ratified. Similar proceedings can be launched by the Governing Body on its own initiative or on the receipt of a complaint from any delegate to the Conference (article 26).

The present chapter will deal with the first two of the above-mentioned procedures, and will also examine certain questions relating to the ratification, entry into force, and denunciation of ILO Conventions. A few words will also be said on the special position with regard to international labour standards of States newly admitted to membership of the ILO.

Submission to the "competent" authorities

When a Convention or Recommendation has been adopted by the Conference, the text of the new "instrument" is sent to all member States so that they may consider applying it. One of the most fundamental obligations imposed on governments by the ILO Constitution is that within 12 or in exceptional cases 18 months the government must then submit both Conventions and Recommendations "to the authority or authorities within whose competence the matter lies, for the enactment of legislation or other action". They must also report back to the ILO on the measures they have taken in that respect and on the action taken by the "competent" authority or authorities. Since the implementation of a Convention or Recommendation normally requires legislation, the "competent authority" (or appropriate body) will in most cases be the national parliament, legislative assembly or congress: it is for that body to decide whether the action of the International Labour Conference should be followed up at national level, by translating the international standards into national legislation.

The position is more complicated in federal States since, under a federal constitution, the central government may not be entitled to make laws on the subject covered by a particular Convention or Recommendation, that being a power of the different constituent states, provinces or cantons that together make up the federal State. In such cases the ILO Constitution also lays down the procedure to be followed. The central government is required to make arrangements for the text to be referred to the legislatures of the constituent units of the federation within 18 months and to report to the Director-General of the ILO on the steps taken and on the results achieved. Where a nation is a federation of many different states, each with substantial power to make its own laws, this can be a long and complicated process. It gets even more complicated if parts of the Convention or Recommendation are a federal responsibility and other parts fall within the competence of the individual states.

When a government places a Convention or Recommendation before the competent legislative authority, it is expected to indicate what action it considers desirable. It may indicate that the instrument is already fully applied in national law and practice and can therefore be ratified or accepted; it may recommend the enactment of legislation to give full effect to the instrument, followed – in the case of a Convention – by ratification; it may recommend that the question of ratification of a Convention should be deferred in order to allow time for the carrying out of consultations or studies on the matter; or it may recommend that a Convention should not be ratified.

Once the submission procedure has been completed, and the steps taken have been communicated to the International Labour Office, the government's immediate obligations arising from the adoption of a new instrument by the Conference are fulfilled. The report to the Office on the action taken is regarded as an important part of the overall procedure, since it is this report that enables the ILO and its supervisory bodies to ensure that the obligation to submit new instruments to the competent authorities is respected. The points on which a government is expected to report are clearly stated in a memorandum concerning submission to the competent authorities which has been adopted by the Governing Body of the ILO. Among other things, the government should indicate which employers' and workers' organisations have been given copies of its report to the ILO.[1]

In this context it is necessary to point out the very clear distinction that must be drawn between submission to the competent authorities and the act of ratification. This is necessary because governments sometimes ask: "Why should we be obliged to submit to our competent authorities Conventions which we do not intend to ratify?" The answer is, of course, that the obligation to submit, as laid down in the ILO Constitution, is general in character, and applies to both Conventions and Recommendations. It does not, however, imply any obligation to propose that a Convention be ratified or a Recommendation accepted: as has been explained above, governments are free to make whatever proposals they wish in this regard. In addition, regardless of whether or not the submission to the legislative body of an ILO Convention is accompanied by a proposal to ratify (and, in effect, submission frequently does constitute the first step towards ratification), the act of submission is intended to serve the purpose of bringing the contents of ILO Conventions and Recommendations to the knowledge of the public. It can thus create an awareness, on important labour and social matters, of the opinion of what is after all a world parliament of governments, employers and workers, i.e. the International Labour Conference; it can stimulate public debate on these matters; it enables trade unions to become involved in this process and to have an influence on the ratification of Conventions and the acceptance of Recommendations; and even if it does not lead to concrete legislative action it can none the less have a sizeable effect on national attitudes and policies.

Reporting on unratified Conventions and on Recommendations

Let us assume that a government has complied with its obligation to submit newly adopted ILO standards to the competent authority or authorities, and that it has been decided in respect of the Convention or Conventions submitted that ratification would not be appropriate. Until 1948, that was the end of the matter as far as a government's obligations under the ILO Constitution were concerned. This was unfortunate for a number of reasons: obstacles to ratification that may exist at the time of submission may disappear some years later in the course of economic and social development; there is also a tendency on the part of many governments to simply forget about a Convention once a decision has been taken not to ratify it.[2] Considerations such as these led in 1946 to the adoption of an amendment to the ILO Constitution, which entered into force in 1948. This amendment (article 19, paragraphs 5, 6 and 7) provides that the Governing Body may call on all member States to report on the position of their law and practice with regard to matters dealt with in an unratified Convention or a Recommendation, the extent to which effect has been given or is proposed to be given to its provisions and, in the case of a Convention, the difficulties which prevent or delay its ratification. Governments can thus periodically reconsider the possibility of ratifying certain Conventions as well as the use that could be made of certain Recommendations.

It would be asking too much of governments to call upon them to re-examine all unratified Conventions and all Recommendations every year; the Governing Body therefore makes a selection. A glance at the records shows that, since 1949, well over 70 Conventions and well over 50 Recommendations have been selected for review.

There is no set pattern for reviewing unratified Conventions. Some are chosen quite frequently; others more rarely. The choice depends on the current importance of the subject and the extent to which circumstances may have changed since the previous review. It has, however, been the consistent policy of the Governing Body to select at frequent intervals the ILO Conventions particularly concerned with the protection of basic human rights. Thus, during the 1949 to 1997 period, forced labour (Convention No. 29) came up five times, freedom of association (Convention No. 87) six times, and the right to organise (Convention No. 98) six times. Equal remuneration (Convention No. 100) was reviewed four times after its adoption in 1951, while discrimination (Convention No. 111) has been reviewed five times since 1958. In addition, the Governing Body decided that governments of all States which have not ratified the Conventions on forced labour (Nos. 29 and 105), freedom of association (Nos. 87 and 98), discrimination (Nos. 100 and 111) and child labour (No. 138) should be asked under article 19 of the Constitution to supply special reports on them in a four-yearly cycle.

In this process of reviewing unratified Conventions and Recommendations from time to time, workers and employers have an important role to play. Their respective groups in the Governing Body can influence the choice of instruments to be selected for reporting; at the national level the principal workers' and employers' organisations are entitled to receive copies of the governments' reports and can comment on them to the ILO; and, as will be seen in the next chapter, their role is no less important when it comes to participating in the ILO's supervisory procedures, an important part of which is designed precisely to check compliance by governments with their reporting obligations.

The Governing Body has often stressed the usefulness of this kind of reporting. It enables the ILO to take stock of the progress made by governments towards the application of unratified Conventions and of Recommendations, and serves as a useful reminder to governments of the existence of the standards in question; it helps to clarify doubts that may exist concerning the scope and requirements of given instruments, and thereby serves to pave the way for further ratifications, or at least fuller implementation; and it can also serve the useful purpose of revealing gaps in the body of international labour standards or drawing attention to cases in which existing standards may need to be revised.

Ratification, entry into force and denunciation of Conventions

Having familiarised ourselves with the procedures governing the submission of newly adopted ILO standards to the competent authority or authorities, and having examined the procedures that may be brought into play in respect of unratified Conventions and of Recommendations, the time is now ripe to look at what happens if the submission procedure should result in a decision to ratify a given ILO Convention.

Conventions are similar to international treaties, specific to the field of labour law, and are subject to ratification. When a member State ratifies a Convention, the country pledges itself to apply the Convention's terms and provisions.

Ratification

It is through the ratification of an ILO Convention that a member State formally undertakes to make the provisions of the Convention effective both in law and practice. Article 19, paragraph 5*(d)*, of the ILO Constitution provides that if the member State "obtains the consent of the authority or authorities within whose competence the matter lies, it will communicate the formal ratification of the Convention to the Director-General and will take such action as may be necessary to make effective the provisions of such Convention". Beyond that, no special requirements are laid down as regards the form in which ratifications should be communicated to the ILO. The important thing is, of course, that the document in question clearly indicates that it constitutes the formal undertaking by a State to give effect to a specified Convention or Conventions and that it is signed by someone with authority to act on behalf of the State concerned.

A point that deserves to be made is that ratifications cannot be accompanied by reservations: in other words a government is not allowed to pick and choose at its own discretion among the Articles of a Convention which it undertakes to apply. On the other hand, the texts of a number of Conventions do in fact provide for certain exclusions, exceptions, or options. In such cases it is often specified that, if a ratifying State wishes to avail itself of such permissive clauses, it has to say so in a declaration made in conjunction with the ratification.

On receipt, ratifications of ILO Conventions are registered by the Director-General, notified to all member States of the Organisation, and communicated to the Secretary-General of the United Nations.

Entry into force

A Convention must formally have entered into force before it can become binding on a ratifying State. Normal practice as regards ILO Conventions is to provide for their entry into force 12 months after registration of the second ratification, and after that for each ratifying State 12 months after registration of its ratification.[3] To give an example, the Tripartite Consultation (International Labour Standards) Convention, 1976 (No. 144), received its first ratification on 15 February 1977 and its second on 16 May, and thus formally entered into force on 16 May 1978. Ratifications registered after 16 May 1977 will come into force 12 months after the date on which they were registered.

Denunciation

Every ILO Convention contains an Article defining the conditions in which States that have ratified it may subsequently denounce it, i.e. declare that they no longer wish to be bound by it. In the case of Conventions adopted since 1928, such denunciation is permitted usually at ten-yearly intervals following the date on which the Convention first came into force. Most denunciations have been the automatic consequence of a State's ratification of a revised, more up-to-date Convention on the same subject. There have, however, also been cases in which a Convention was denounced simply because for some reason the State concerned considered itself unable (or no longer able) to give effect to it, or because it considered that the Convention was no longer in accordance with its views or concerns. Such denunciations have been rare: the total was 85 on 1 February 1998, i.e. not even 1 per cent of the total number of ratifications, which currently exceeds 6,500. None the less, the Governing Body has expressed its concern about this type of denunciation and has stated that when the denunciation of a Convention is contemplated it would be desirable for the government concerned, before taking a decision on the matter, to consult fully the representative employers' and workers' organisations on the problems encountered and the measures to be taken to resolve them. This is yet another example of the importance of the role to be played by workers' organisations in the ILO's standard-setting activities.[4]

New member States

Before we conclude this chapter a few words should be said regarding the position with regard to international labour standards of States newly admitted to membership of the ILO.

Such a State must formally accept the obligations of the ILO Constitution; this obligation is considered to include the recognition of certain fundamental principles such as freedom of association and non-discrimination. But what about the vast body of Conventions and Recommendations adopted by the ILO before the new Member joined?

It would be unrealistic to expect a new member State to embark immediately on an examination of all the texts and a programme of legislation that might take several years, perhaps to the exclusion of many other important matters. In point of fact, however, there is usually not so much of a problem. In the case of former colonial territories, a number of ILO Conventions will almost certainly have been applied in the country in question under the special procedure laid. down in the ILO Constitution for "non-metropolitan territories".[5] Under this procedure member States are required to make a declaration in respect of each Convention they ratify, indicating the extent to which they undertake to apply the Convention in each of the non-metropolitan territories for which they are responsible. In the case of non-metropolitan territories that are internally self-governing, the decision on whether a "declaration of application" should be made is for the government of the territory, the formal declaration being made by the member State on its behalf. A declaration of application can be made with such modifications of the provisions of the Convention as may be necessary to adapt it to local conditions.

In the case of new member States whose territory previously comprised part of the territory of another ILO member State, an examination has to be made of which Conventions will continue to be binding by virtue of *state succession*, and which others the new member State wishes to continue to apply and to ratify on becoming independent and joining the ILO.

There is generally, in either case, a basic block of Conventions which have previously been applicable, and the new member State has generally committed itself to the same Conventions, in so far as they remain relevant. This has meant that many former colonial territories (e.g. Namibia), or States previously considered part of the former Soviet Union (e.g. Azerbaijan, Belarus, Estonia, Latvia, Lithuania and Ukraine) or States such as the Czech Republic, Croatia and Slovenia, for example, have commenced (or recommenced) their ILO membership and independent nationhood with a solid foundation in international labour standards.

Notes

[1] The Tripartite Consultation (International Labour Standards) Convention, 1976 (No. 144), carries the participation of employers and workers in the submission procedure an important step further by providing (Article 5, 1*(b)*) for tripartite consultation, on "the proposals to be made to the competent authority or authorities in connection with the submission of Conventions and Recommendations pursuant to article 19 of the Constitution of the International Labour Organisation".

[2] This is the main reason why the Tripartite Consultation (International Labour Standards) Convention, 1976 (No. 144), provides (Article 5, 1*(c)*) that one of the subjects of the consultations should be "the re-examination at appropriate intervals of unratified Conventions and of Recommendations to which effect has not yet been given, to consider what measures might be taken to promote their implementation and ratification as appropriate".

[3] Some Conventions, e.g. certain maritime Conventions, require a higher number of ratifications before their initial entry into force.

[4] A State that has ratified the Tripartite Consultation (International Labour Standards) Convention, 1976 (No. 144), will be under a formal obligation to consult the most representative workers' and employers' organisations on "proposals for the denunciation of ratified Conventions" (Article 5, 1(e)).

[5] The procedure in question is set out in article 35 of the ILO Constitution. In 1964 the Conference adopted an amendment to the Constitution which has not yet entered into force. This amendment provides for the deletion of article 35 and the substitution in article 19 of the Constitution of provisions concerning the acceptance of Conventions in respect of territories for whose international relations a member State is responsible.

Points for discussion

1. Describe the obligations of member States of the ILO as regards the submission of Conventions and Recommendations to the competent national authorities.
2. What role can workers' organisations play in these procedures?
3. What is the objective of reporting on unratified Conventions and on Recommendations, and what is the significance of this exercise for workers?
4. What are the effects of ratification?
5. Describe the role of workers' organisations in the case of denunciation of Conventions.
6. What is the position of newly independent States as regards the application of Conventions?

Further reading

ILO: *Trade union participation in implementing international labour standards*, course topic, Geneva, 1994, available from the Bureau for Workers' Activities.

Chapter 6

General application of standards: (II) Supervision and assistance

In the previous chapter we saw how governments are required to submit newly adopted Conventions and Recommendations to the competent authorities, and how reports are subsequently requested from time to time on the position in national law and practice as regards unratified Conventions as well as Recommendations. In this chapter, we shall examine the normal supervisory procedure by which the ILO seeks to ensure the observance by governments of their obligations in the above respects. Above all, however, we shall concern ourselves with the obligations of governments in respect of Conventions which they have ratified, with the normal supervisory procedures designed to ensure observance of such obligations, and with certain procedures or activities of the ILO which supplement its regular supervisory machinery. First of all, however, let us consider for a moment an important question of principle which poses itself as regards the whole concept of international supervision.

International relations and national sovereignty

One of the distinctive features of international labour Conventions is that they are international treaties, but at the same time primarily concerned with matters that were long considered to be solely the concern of each individual State. In fact, treaties such as the Conventions adopted by the International Labour Conference since 1919 represent something entirely new in the sphere of international treaty-making, because they require a sovereign State that ratifies them to guarantee certain social, labour or human rights to its own citizens as well as to foreigners residing on its territory.[1] This affects the whole traditional concept of national sovereignty, since it acknowledges the principle that there is in this field an international law whose authority transcends frontiers. How, then, can this principle be made effective?

One suggestion that has sometimes been made is that there should be international inspectors with rights of entry and investigation, and international courts with jurisdiction over the matters in question. Today, many believe that the chances that such a system would be accepted by States are rather remote, while others argue that it could happen, at least in part, as certain initiatives in the field of child labour in the 1990s appear to indicate. In 1947 Professor Scelle, a French authority on international law, proposed that the ILO should have "representatives" in member States who would not themselves have the authority of inspectors, but would be permanently associated in some way with the national inspection services and would report to Geneva. The vote in the Conference committee that considered the Professor's proposal was 8 in favour (all Workers) and 29 against, with 4 abstentions. Three Workers' delegates were among the opponents. Less far-reaching suggestions have been made from time to time – for example that countries might voluntarily establish contacts between their inspection services and the International Labour Office – but so far none of these ideas have come to fruition.

In his Report to the 1994 Session of the Conference, entitled *Defending values, promoting change,* the Director-General invited reflection on how to strengthen the authority of the ILO as regards the promotion and supervision of basic social rights. The Workers' group wanted similar supervision of forced labour and equal opportunities as is exercised by the Governing Body Committee on Freedom of Association with respect to freedom of association. This idea did not receive the approval of the other groups. At the 1997 Session of the Conference, the Director-General proposed the idea of a solemn declaration of fundamental workers' rights, for discussion at a future session, in order to give a stronger basis to new mechanisms of supervision. Such supervision would be carried out by an existing ILO body. Such a declaration adopted by the Conference might help to define the universally acknowledged content of the fundamental rights that should be respected by all Members of the ILO, irrespective of whether or not they have ratified the corresponding Conventions, and to establish a mechanism to guarantee their promotion.

Regular supervision

Whatever ideal solutions the future may hold, the ILO has sought from the outset to establish methods of supervision that would work and would be acceptable to its member States. In this way a system of supervision by consent has gradually been evolved. Two complementary approaches have been followed: first, the ILO Constitution contains provisions under which governments have to report to the ILO (a) on the measures taken to submit newly adopted standards to the competent authorities, (b) on the position of their national law and practice with regard to unratified Conventions and to Recommendations, and (c) on the measures taken to give effect to ratified Conventions. Secondly, if international supervision is to be meaningful, governments' reports have to be carefully examined and evaluated. Since 1927 this task has been carried out each year in the first instance by a Committee of Experts on the Application of Conventions and Recommendations, and subsequently at the annual session of the International Labour Conference, where the report of the Committee of Experts is examined by a special tripartite Conference committee.

The key elements of regular ILO supervision are thus the communication of government reports and their examination. We will now examine how the system works in practice.

Government reports

Governments' reporting obligations as regards submission to the competent authorities, as well as in respect of unratified Conventions and of Recommendations, were dealt with in the preceding chapter. Here we shall concern ourselves essentially with the obligation to supply reports on the effect given to ratified Conventions. In this respect, article 22 of the ILO Constitution provides that each member State shall "make an annual report to the International Labour Office on the measures which it has taken to give effect to the provisions of Conventions to which it is a party. These reports shall be made in such form and shall contain such particulars as the Governing Body may request". It will be seen that this important constitutional provision regulates two distinct matters, namely the periodicity and the contents of governments' reports. Let us deal with the two matters in succession.

Originally, the constitutional requirements that reports on ratified Conventions should be submitted every year did not give rise to serious difficulties. When the Committee of Experts first met in 1927, it was called upon to examine some 150 reports. By the end of the 1950s the number of ratifications had risen to almost 2,000, and the system of reporting and of examining reports received was placing an increasingly heavy burden on both governments and the ILO. In 1959, therefore, the Governing Body decided that detailed reports from governments should as a rule be called for only once every two years. By 1976 the situation had again become difficult, the number of ILO Conventions having risen to over 140, the total number of member States to over 130, the total number of ratifications to well over 4,000, and the number of reports due to about 3,400. Measures were again urgently required, both to ease the burden of reporting placed on governments and to reduce the workload of the supervisory bodies, while at the same time ensuring that the effectiveness of the supervisory machinery was not jeopardised. As from 1977 further changes have therefore been made in the system of reporting.

In November 1993 the Governing Body approved a series of new changes to the system of reporting, which came into force in 1996 for a trial period of five years. A first *detailed* report is requested the year after a Convention comes into force in a given country. A second *detailed* report is requested two years later (or one year, if that is the year when a periodic report is in any event due from all countries bound by that Convention).

Subsequent reports are requested periodically on one of the following bases, on the understanding that the Committee of Experts on the Application of Conventions and Recommendations may request detailed reports outside the normal periodicity:

(i) *Detailed* reports are automatically requested every two years on the following ten *priority Conventions*:

- *freedom of association:* Nos. 87 and 98;
- *abolition of forced labour:* Nos. 29 and 105;
- *equal treatment and opportunities:* Nos. 100 and 111;
- *employment policy:* No. 122;
- *labour inspection:* Nos. 81 and 129;
- *tripartite consultation:* No. 144.

(ii) *Simplified* reports are requested every five years on other Conventions. A *detailed* report is nevertheless required:

— where the Committee of Experts has made an observation or direct request calling for a reply; or

— where the Committee of Experts considers that a *detailed* report should be communicated because of possible changes in legislation or practice in a member State which might affect its application of the Convention.

Non-periodic *detailed* reports on the application of a ratified Convention are required:

(i) when the Committee of Experts or the Conference Committee on the Application of Standards so requests;

(ii) when the Committee of Experts is asked to consider the follow-up to proceedings instituted under articles 24 or 26 of the Constitution or before the Committee on Freedom of Association;

(iii) when comments have been received from national or international employers' or workers' organisations and the Committee of Experts considers that a detailed report is warranted in the light of the government's comments in reply or the fact that the government has not replied;

(iv) when no report is supplied or no reply is given to comments made by the supervisory bodies (given that, where there is repeated failure to reply or the reply is manifestly inadequate, the Committee of Experts may examine the matter on the basis of available information).

Subject to the conditions and safeguards laid down by the Governing Body, no reports are requested on Conventions which do not correspond to present-day needs (namely Conventions Nos. 15, 20, 21, 28, 34-40, 43, 48, 49, 50, 60, 64, 65, 67, 86 and 104).

Annual *general* reports are no longer requested under article 22.

Each report on a ratified Convention has to be supplied on the basis of a report form which is approved by the Governing Body, and which contains the substantive provisions of the Convention and a number of questions on how it is applied, both in law and in practice. The first point which the governments' reports should establish is whether the law complies with the provisions of the Convention. For a Convention that requires the establishment of administrative or other machinery, the practical arrangements made must be described, and particulars of their operation given. For a promotional Convention,[2] the report must describe the measures taken toward the achievement of the goal of the Convention and to overcome any obstacles in the way of its full application. If any decisions of principle have been made by courts of law or other tribunals relating to the application of the Convention, details are required. A general description of the manner in which the Convention is applied in practice is then expected, with extracts from inspectors' reports, information about the number of contraventions, and so on. Finally, governments must indicate the organisations of employers and workers to which copies of its report have been sent, and whether any observations have been received from such organisations. The government's obligation to communicate copies to the recognised representative organisations of its report on the implementation of international labour standards is laid in down in article 23, paragraph 2, of the ILO Constitution.

The Committee of Experts

The examination of governments' reports is carried out in the first instance by the Committee of Experts on the Application of Conventions and Recommendations. At present the Committee consists of 20 independent persons of the highest standing, with eminent qualifications in the legal or social fields and with an intimate knowledge of labour conditions or administration. Members of the Committee are drawn from all parts of the world. They are appointed by the Governing Body of the ILO on the proposals of the Director-General, in their personal capacity, for a period of three years, their term of office being renewable for successive periods of three years. They meet each year in March in Geneva.

It has been said that independence and objectivity are the life-breath of the international judicial inquiry. This saying is fully applicable to the functions and responsibilities of the Committee of Experts. In this connection it may be useful to quote the words used by the Committee of Experts itself when it reaffirmed its belief in this fundamental principle in 1977:

The Committee's fundamental principles, as voiced on a number of occasions, call for impartiality and objectivity in pointing out the extent to which it appears that the position in each State is in conformity with the terms of the Conventions and the obligations which that State has undertaken by virtue of the Constitution of the ILO. The members of the Committee must accomplish their task in complete independence as regards all member States.

In essence, the functions of the Committee of Experts can be grouped under three headings: the examination of governments' reports on the application of ratified Conventions; the examination of governments' reports on the situation in national law and practice as regards selected unratified Conventions and Recommendations; and the examination of information supplied by governments as regards submission of newly adopted Conventions and Recommendations to the competent authorities.

In examining the effect given to ratified Conventions, the Committee of Experts is not limited to the information provided by governments. Information on a country's legislation can usually be found in official gazettes and similar publications where laws and regulations are printed. Other documentation available to the Committee may include the texts of collective agreements or court decisions, the conclusions of other ILO bodies such as commissions of inquiry and the Governing Body Committee on Freedom of Association, and comments made by employers' or workers' organisations. Such comments may either be included by the government with its report, or addressed directly to the ILO by the organisation concerned. In the latter case the Office sends a copy of the observations to the government in question, so that the Committee can also consider any comment the government may wish to add in reply. The comments by workers' organisations on the application of ratified Conventions and, in general, on any other subject covered by governments' reports in the field of international labour standards are of great importance. They enable workers to participate fully in the supervisory system of the ILO, almost continuously and at any time, and thus to contribute to a fuller implementation of international labour standards, as well as to contribute to improving the working and living conditions of workers.

If the Committee finds that a government is not fully complying with the requirements of a ratified Convention, or with its constitutional obligations regarding Conventions and Recommendations, it addresses a comment to that government, drawing attention to the shortcomings and requesting that steps be taken to eliminate them. The Committee's comment may take the form of -

(a) observations, which are published in its report and which are used for the more serious or long-standing cases of failure to comply with obligations, and are also normally used when a workers' or employers' organisation has sent in comments on the application of a ratified Convention which require to be followed up; or

(b) direct requests, which are not published but are sent direct to the governments concerned, and to workers' and employers' organisations in the country concerned for information.

Direct requests are usually made when a minor discrepancy is involved, or when the government has not made available sufficient information to enable the Committee of Experts to assess the way in which a ratified Convention is applied. These requests, together with the observations appearing in the Committee's published report, are sent to the government for reply together with the regular request for a report on the application of the Convention concerned.

The Committee's observations are clear and to the point. They are also thorough, usually running each year to a printed book longer than this manual. Here is an example of a comment on the application of the Freedom of Association and Protection of the Right to Organise Convention, 1948 (No. 87):

> The Committee notes that the Government has recently placed the trade union organisations under its control, and has temporarily suspended the activities of employers' and workers' organisations except as regards their internal administration and their social activities. The Committee trusts that the Government will proceed at the earliest possible date with a normalisation of the trade union situation and will adopt new legislation in the field in full harmony with the standards contained in the Convention.

Other observations illustrate the effect of previous comments of the Committee. An entry relating to the Night Work of Young Persons (Industry) Convention (Revised), 1948 (No. 90), was as follows:

> Further to its earlier observations, the Committee notes with satisfaction that section 15 of the new Labour Code prohibits night work in industry for young persons under 18 years of age between 6 p.m. and 7 a.m., thus giving effect to the Convention.

The reports supplied by governments on the situation of national law and practice, in respect of unratified Conventions and of Recommendations selected by the Governing Body for reporting each year, provide the basis for the carrying out by the Committee of Experts of a general survey. As was mentioned in the preceding chapter, the reports and general surveys are of considerable value, since they often help to clarify doubts concerning the scope or requirements of a Convention or Recommendation, sometimes serve to pave the way for further ratifications, and may also serve the useful purpose of identifying gaps in the body of international labour standards or instances in which existing standards may need to be revised. They are also of great importance for workers' organisations, providing them with a picture and guide-lines regarding the overall situation in the world on each particular subject.

However, in his Report to the 81st Session of the International Labour Conference, entitled *Defending values, promoting change* (Geneva, 1994), the Director-General considered that general surveys are not really an ideal vehicle for evaluation, and should therefore be reoriented towards an audit of existing standards and of the advisability of maintaining them (pages 49-50).

The Committee of Experts also examines the extent to which governments have complied with their obligations under article 19 of the Constitution to submit to the competent authorities instruments adopted by the International Labour Conference. The findings in this regard are included in the Committee's report. As in the case of ratified Conventions, the Committee's comments take the form of observations (in more serious cases of non-compliance) or direct requests.

The Conference Committee

The report of the Committee of Experts is submitted to each annual session of the International Labour Conference, where it is examined and discussed by an especially appointed tripartite Conference committee on the application of Conventions and Recommendations. Since it is at this stage of the ILO's supervision procedure that the trade union representatives play what is perhaps their major role, let us look in some detail at the proceedings of this committee.

The committee usually comprises well over 150 members from the three groups of delegates and advisers (governments, employers, workers); usually there is not an equal number of government, employers' and workers' representatives on the committee, and votes are therefore weighted so as to ensure equality of voting strength for the three groups. The committee traditionally elects a Government member as its chairman, as well as two vice-chairmen, one of whom is an Employer representative, the other representing the Workers' group.

Each year the committee begins its work with a general discussion, in which it reviews a number of broad issues relating to the ratification and application of ILO standards and the compliance by member States in general with their obligation under the ILO Constitution with regard to these standards. In this context the committee also discusses the Committee of Experts' General Survey of national law and practice in regard to instruments which have been the subject of reports under article 19 of the Constitution, i.e. reports on unratified Conventions and on Recommendations.

After its general discussion, the committee then turns to an examination of individual cases. Governments which have been mentioned in the Committee of Experts' report as not complying with their obligations under the ILO Constitution, or not fully applying a ratified Convention, may be invited to make a statement to the Conference committee on the application of Conventions and Recommendations. There is no formal obligation to do so, but they rarely decline. Some circulate written statements; in many cases their representative appears personally before the committee. If the committee is not satisfied with a written reply, it gives governments an opportunity to supply fuller information orally. Government representatives may not always find this an easy task, but they know that the committee takes a positive attitude. Its object is not to apportion blame, but to obtain results. Government spokesmen making statements usually explain frankly their difficulties in applying a particular standard and indicate the steps they propose to take to overcome them. The spectacle of the delegate of a country being politely questioned about his or her government's application of international labour standards by a workers' representative from the other end of the world, and responding courteously and frankly in the process, often comes as something of a revelation to people attending a sitting of the committee for the first time. The record shows that such factual exchanges, based on the technical findings of the Committee of Experts, help to maintain momentum towards better compliance with standards.

The discussions on individual cases are summarised in the annexes to the report which the committee submits to the Conference. In addition, in the Committee's general report the attention of the Conference is specially drawn to the most serious cases in which governments have failed to comply with their reporting obligations under articles 19, 22 and 23 of the Constitution, or with their obligation to implement ratified Conventions fully. Where explanations were given on the difficulties encountered by the governments concerned, those explanations are also briefly mentioned in the general report.

The committee's report is submitted to the Conference, which discusses it in one or more plenary sittings. This discussion provides delegates from all the three groups with an opportunity to draw further attention to particular aspects of the committee's work. Once adopted by the Conference, the report is dispatched to governments, their special attention being drawn to points which they should take into account in the preparation of their next reports to the ILO.

Assistance to member States

This concludes our examination of the ILO's routine procedure for the supervision of the application of international labour standards, a procedure which works largely on the assumption that governments are acting in good faith and which depends to a considerable extent on persuasion and publicity. In the following chapters, we shall turn to what are sometimes called "special" supervision procedures, which fall under two broad headings: (a) representations and complaints procedures under the ILO Constitution; and (b) special machinery for supervising freedom of association. Before doing so, however, it might be useful to look at some of the practical ways in which the ILO tries to help member States that are having difficulties in applying international labour standards. These different types of action constitute a valuable supplement to the ILO's regular supervision machinery; the procedure of direct contacts and the work of the regional advisers for international labour standards have grown directly out of the regular supervision process.

Direct contacts

We have seen how the ILO's system of regular supervision consists essentially of a dialogue between the member States, on the one hand, and the supervisory bodies, on the other. Indications in the governments' reports give rise to comments by the Committee of Experts, which are discussed in the Conference committee and to which governments are able to reply in their next reports. And so the dialogue continues. Experience has shown, however, that the continuation of this dialogue, sometimes over a prolonged period, has at times failed to lead to the desired results. In certain cases, the government in question may contest year after year the experts' assessment of the effect of its laws and of the factual situation prevailing in the country. In other cases, the government may contest the experts' view as to the exact meaning of a Convention or the compatibility or incompatibility of the national situation with the Convention. The situation that arises most frequently, however, is one in which even if the experts' views are not contested, no action is taken to remedy the shortcomings, so that year after year the supervisory bodies find it necessary to repeat their comments without success.

It was in the light of such situations, which created a deadlock equally frustrating to all the parties concerned, that the Committee of Experts suggested, in 1968, that there should be more direct contacts between a government and a representative of the Director-General of the ILO. A procedure established for this purpose has been in operation since 1969. The results achieved through this procedure, which can obviously be followed only with the full consent of the government concerned, have been positive in a number of countries. The direct contacts involve a visit to the country in question and informal discussions of the discrepancies noted or the difficulties encountered with government representatives having the necessary degree of experience, responsibility and authority. A further principle, endorsed by the Committee of Experts and already applied in practice, concerns the desirability of associating employers' and workers' organisations with the direct contacts, by keeping them informed of the topics discussed and by eliciting their points of view. During the discussion on the application of international labour standards at the International Labour Conference, workers' organisations may also suggest direct contacts to the government concerned.

Seminars and other types of training

Other means of action, of an educational nature and with a direct bearing on international labour standards, should also be mentioned. Since 1964, regional seminars on national and international labour standards have been held every year or two in different parts of the world for senior government officials who are directly responsible in their countries for the administration of matters concerning compliance with obligations under the ILO Constitution relating to standards. The seminars have proved to be a very useful means of training such officials with a view to a better discharge of their responsibilities in questions related to standards. The second type of training is directed to the workers: since 1968 some short study courses on ILO standards have been run, sometimes just before sessions of the general or regional conferences of the Organisation. The purpose of these latter courses is to familiarise workers' representatives attending these meetings, particularly those attending a standards-related discussion for the first time, with the machinery and procedures existing with regard to standards, thus enabling them to play a full and active part in the proceedings. Tripartite seminars have also been organised at the regional, subregional and national levels, and fellowships are granted for training at ILO headquarters in Geneva.

In addition, the ILO offers several courses on different subjects: the objectives of the ILO, its structure, tripartism in practice, the procedures for adoption and the content of international labour standards, employment and development, the activities of multinational enterprises, workers' education, technical cooperation, etc. The aim of these courses is to give trade unionists information and direction which would allow them to participate effectively in ILO activities, in particular in the field of international labour standards.

Standards specialists

Many multidisciplinary teams include specialists in international labour standards. These senior ILO officials are called upon to assist governments to fulfil their constitutional obligations as regards labour standards, by visiting the countries concerned and organising national and regional seminars on the question. They are sometimes asked to make the direct contacts described above.

The Active Partnership Policy

This policy aims to bring the ILO closer to its constituents and thereby to improve the quality of its services to member States. It allows objectives to be set on the spot, country by country. It is the directors of area offices who establish the selection of priorities, with support from the multidisciplinary teams. The ILO, through its multidisciplinary teams, establishes programmes which take into account the specificities of each country and the requirements of the tripartite constituents. This policy depends heavily upon close collaboration between the multidisciplinary teams, the directors of area offices and the technical departments at headquarters in Geneva. The regional offices' mission are to provide assistance to the area offices and the multidisciplinary teams and to determine regional priorities. The directors of regional offices supervise the activities of the area offices and the multidisciplinary teams. The formulation of country objectives is completed after consultations in which representatives of workers, employers and government participate. An action programme is elaborated, implemented and followed through in collaboration with the social partners. The Active Partnership Policy has facilitated enhanced application of tripartite principles.

At present there are 16 multidisciplinary teams around the world, which provide consultative services and technical assistance in a variety of fields, helping the technical co-operation programmes to achieve their objectives.

Knowledge and understanding of the priorities of each country allow the ILO to meet member States' needs more effectively. Proximity to government, employers' and workers' representatives on a day-to-day basis builds links of mutual confidence and allows better understanding of the social problems of the countries concerned. This policy aims to reinforce the ILO's action on its mandate, which is to advance towards social justice, to combat poverty and to promote employment.

Technical co-operation

A few words must also be said about the relationship between the ILO's operational and standard-setting activities. The past 30 years have seen a vast expansion of the ILO's technical co-operation activities. At the same time, a parallel trend has become equally noticeable: the general agreement throughout the Organisation on the need for effective co-ordination between operational and standard-setting activities, if these two major means of ILO action are to develop, as they should, into mutually interdependent and mutually reinforcing activities.

Within the International Labour Office there are well-established procedures to ensure that the necessary co-ordination is achieved. Technical co-operation experts are supplied with written and oral instructions to make them as familiar as possible with the situation as regards the ratification and application of standards in their country of assignment, with special emphasis laid on any standards, whether ratified or not, that may have a bearing on the subject-matter of their assignment. The advice or recommendations which an expert puts forward should not be in conflict with the provisions of a ratified Convention. Standards on basic human rights – such as those on freedom of association, freedom from forced labour and freedom from discrimination in employment and occupation – should be taken into account even in the absence of ratification. Under the same instructions, the final report on a project – in the preparation of which all the units concerned in the Office co-operate – must refer to its standard-setting implications, including in particular any remedial action that may be required.

In addition, the Committee of Experts on the Application of Conventions and Recommendations is well aware of the need to establish a link between standards and technical co-operation. It therefore draws attention from time to time in its annual reports to specific cases where, in its view, the application of ratified Conventions could be facilitated through technical co-operation, and these cases are subsequently brought to the attention of the appropriate technical departments within the Office.

Notes

[1] In fact, a beginning had already been made in 1906, as stated in Chapter 1, when a diplomatic conference held in Berne had adopted two Conventions, one of which prohibited night work by women in industry and the other the use of white phosphorus in the manufacture of matches.

[2] See Chapter 3.

Points for discussion

1. What does the regular supervision of the ILO consist of?
2. Describe the role of workers' organisations in the various stages of regular supervision.
3. Does your trade union make use of the possibility to comment on the implementation of international labour standards in your country? Give recent examples.
4. Describe the ILO's assistance to member States in the field of international labour standards and the possibility of workers' participation in its various forms.
5. Explain the practical meaning of article 23, paragraph 2, of the ILO Constitution.

Group exercise

Form three groups representing government, workers' and employers' members of the Conference committee on the application of Conventions and Recommendations and try to discuss a subject concerning the implementation of international labour standards.

Further reading

ILO: *Trade union participation in the ILO supervisory system for the protection of trade union rights*, course topic, Geneva, 1994, available from the Bureau for Workers' Activities.

Nicolas Valticos: "Once more about the ILO system of supervision: In what respect is it still a model?", in N. Blokker and S. Muller (eds.): *Towards more effective supervision by international organizations*, Dordrecht, Boston and London, Martinus Nijhoff Publications, 1994.

It would also be useful to consult a *Report of the Committee of Experts on the Application of Conventions and Recommendations*, such as the one for 1997, which contains a general survey on the Labour Administration Convention (No. 150) and Recommendation (No. 158), 1978.

Chapter 7

Representations and complaints

The ILO relies primarily on the regular procedures described in Chapter 6 in supervising the application of Conventions and Recommendations. However, the ILO Constitution also provides for two procedures for the examination of specific allegations that the provisions of a ratified Convention are not being effectively observed in a particular case, namely the procedure of representations and the procedure of complaints.

Representations

The representations procedure is governed by articles 24 and 25 of the ILO Constitution as well as by a set of rules adopted by the Governing Body. In essence, the procedure works as follows. Any employers' or workers' organisation, national or international, can make a so-called representation to the ILO if it considers that a given member State has failed to apply in any respect the effective observance within its jurisdiction of any Convention which it has ratified. The Governing Body may communicate this representation to the government concerned for its comments. If no such comments are received within a reasonable time or if the comments received are considered to be unsatisfactory, the Governing Body may publish the representation and the government's reply. In doing so, the Governing Body in its conclusions also indicates in what respects it considers any issues raised by the representation to have been satisfactorily disposed of or, on the contrary, to require either further action or clarification. In practice, the examination of representation is carried out by a committee composed of three members of the Governing Body (chosen respectively from among the Government, Employer and Worker members), which reports to the Governing Body itself.

Complaints

The ILO Constitution (articles 26-29 and 31-34) also provides for a considerably more elaborate procedure for the examination of complaints. Under this procedure any member State may file a complaint with the ILO if it is not satisfied that another member State is securing the effective observance of any Convention which both have ratified. Similar proceedings may be initiated by the Governing Body, either on its own or on receipt of a complaint from a delegate (Government, Employer or Worker) to the International Labour Conference.

When a complaint has been received, the Governing Body may appoint a commission of inquiry to examine the case. Such commissions are composed of three prominent persons appointed in a personal capacity. The quasi-judicial nature of their proceedings and the full independence in which they are expected to function are reflected in the fact that their members are requested to make a solemn declaration in which they undertake "to perform their duties and exercise their powers honourably, faithfully, impartially and conscientiously". The ILO Constitution further provides that if a commission of inquiry is set up all member States, whether directly concerned in the complaint or not, are to place at the disposal of the commission all the information in their possession which bears on the subject-matter of the complaint. After fully considering the complaint, the commission is required to prepare a report embodying its findings on all questions of fact relevant to determining the issue between the parties, and containing its recommendations concerning what should be done in response to the complaint. Beyond the above, there are no hard and fast rules governing the procedure to be followed by commissions of inquiry. The cases examined have mostly been so difficult and controversial that unduly rigid instructions from the Governing Body might have made it difficult if not impossible for the commission to achieve positive results. The Governing Body has recognised that a commission of inquiry should not only examine whatever information may be submitted by or in support of the parties but should itself take all necessary steps to ensure that it has at its disposal thorough and objective information concerning the questions at issue; and it has been left to the commissions themselves to determine their own procedure on the basis of the relevant provisions in the ILO Constitution and general directives issued by the Governing Body.

The commissions of inquiry undertake a thorough examination of all issues of fact and law; they call for statements and documentary evidence from the parties; extend invitations to make similar submissions to countries bordering on the countries or territories involved in the complaint or having important trade relations with them, as well as to various non-governmental organisations (particularly international organisations of workers and employers); proceed to hear witnesses some of whom appear at the commission's own initiative whereas others are heard at the request of parties. In the vast majority of cases, the commissions supplement the hearings by on-the-spot investigations.

On completion, the report of a commission of inquiry is communicated to the Governing Body and to each of the governments concerned in the complaint, and is also published. Each of the governments concerned is allowed a period of three months in which to indicate whether or not it accepts the recommendations made in the commission's report. A government that does not accept the recommendations is entitled to refer the complaint to the International Court of Justice. The Court can then affirm, vary or reserve the commission's findings or recommendations, and its decision on the matter is final.

A final noteworthy aspect of the procedure is that commissions of inquiry couple their recommendations with a request to the governments concerned to provide indications in their regular reports to the ILO on the steps they have taken to give effect to the recommendations in question. In this way a link is established between the special complaints procedure and the normal supervisory procedure, and the Committee of Experts and the Conference committee on the application of Conventions and Recommendations can then examine at regular intervals the measures taken and the progress made by governments in this regard.

Usefulness of representations and complaints procedures

The representations and complaints procedures have not been used often, although the number of cases has tended to increase in recent years. The limited use made of the procedures in question is probably largely due to the fact that in the great majority of cases the regular supervisory machinery based on the examination of reports by the

Committee of Experts and the Conference committee meets the needs. In the preceding chapter we saw how important a role employers' and workers' organisations can play in this connection, both by submitting comments on the reports submitted by their governments and by participating in the work of the Conference committee. On the whole, these organisations have no doubt considered active participation along such lines in the supervisory process to be preferable to the use of more formal constitutional procedures. As far as governments are concerned, the limited number of complaints lodged under article 26 of the Constitution is perhaps to be explained by the fact that member States hesitate to put forward complaints, both because of the unfriendly character such a gesture might be considered to have and because of the risk that complaints might lead to reprisals in the form of counter-complaints.

Nevertheless, it is useful that procedures of an exceptional nature such as those described in this chapter exist as a sort of last resort in cases in which the regular supervisory machinery has appeared inadequate and a more thorough examination has seemed necessary. It is even essential, when serious disagreements occur on the application of ratified Conventions (most frequently those dealing with fundamental human rights and sometimes in a delicate or difficult political context), that the ILO should have at its disposal procedures offering guarantees of an impartial and meticulous examination. These can give the parties concerned the confidence that is necessary if they are to co-operate fully in the proceedings and accept the conclusions that emerge.

Ad hoc studies and investigations

We have described the arrangements that enable the ILO to receive and examine allegations of non-compliance with ratified Conventions, and we shall describe in the next chapter the procedures for the examination of alleged infringements of trade union rights. Special (ad hoc) inquiries or studies, either of a general scope or in relation to particular countries, have also been undertaken from time to time. These special inquiries or studies, which have been based on existing ILO standards, have been carried out to throw light on controversial issues, to prepare the way for possible further ILO action, and to assist governments in the consideration and solution of current social problems. They have mostly been concerned with forced labour or freedom of association.

Among inquiries of a general scope, those undertaken by a United Nations-ILO Ad Hoc Committee on Forced Labour and an ILO Committee on Forced Labour between 1951 and 1959 deserve special mention. These forced labour inquiries helped to bring about radical changes of policy and practice in a significant number of countries, and also led to the adoption by the International Labour Conference in 1957 of the Abolition of Forced Labour Convention (No. 105). In the field of freedom of association, a committee composed of independent persons under the chairmanship of Lord McNair, a former president of the International Court of Justice, carried out in 1955-56 an important inquiry into the extent of freedom of employers' and workers' organisations from government domination or control.

There have also been several studies or inquiries relating to the situation in specific countries. To take one example only, in 1967 a study group composed of three independent persons was set up by the Governing Body to examine the labour and trade union situation in Spain. This was done at the request of the Government of Spain, which at that time had not ratified the ILO Conventions on freedom of association. In July 1969 the study group submitted its final report, containing a detailed description and evaluation of the labour and trade union situation in Spain. This report was an important element in the discussions and changes which followed, leading in the spring of 1977 to the adoption of a new trade union law giving substantial effect to the provisions of Conventions Nos. 87 and 98 and then the ratification of the two Conventions by Spain.

Points for discussion

1. Describe the possibilities that workers' organisations have to participate in the representations and complaints procedures.
2. Has your trade union organisation already made a representation? Has your Workers' delegate to the International Labour Conference already filed a complaint?
3. In your opinion, what is the usefulness for trade unions of the representations and complaints procedures?

Further reading

ILO: *Trade unions and the ILO,* A workers' education manual, second (revised) edition, Geneva, 1988.

ILO: *Trade union participation in the ILO supervisory system for the protection of trade union rights*, course topic, Geneva, 1994, available from the Bureau for Workers' Activities.

Chapter 8

Protecting freedom of association and other trade union rights

Freedom of association provides workers with the right to form their own trade unions or organisations and to join them freely, and guarantees that these organisations will be able to function without interference from the public authorities.

Trade union rights, constituting an integral part of human rights, are a combination of all the rights and freedoms which are essential for the existence, and the efficient functioning, of democratic trade unions capable of defending and furthering the interests of workers.

Freedom of association has a unique place among the basic human rights and freedoms of concern to the ILO. It is a prerequisite for progress towards social justice; it enables the workers to give expression to their aspirations; it strengthens their position in collective bargaining, by re-establishing a balance in the strength of the parties; it constitutes a healthy counterweight to the power of the State, by enabling labour to participate in the framing and carrying out of economic and social policies; and, last but not least, it is essential for the proper functioning of an organisation like the ILO based on tripartism, that is to say co-operation on an equal footing between workers, employers and governments. In addition to being acknowledged as a fundamental principle in the Preamble to the ILO Constitution and reaffirmed, together with the principle of freedom of expression, in the Declaration of Philadelphia, freedom of association is prominent among the subjects dealt with in a number of texts adopted by the International Labour Conference. In previous chapters we examined the history of the standard-setting process and also described the contents of the Freedom of Association and Protection of the Right to Organise Convention, 1948 (No. 87), and the Right to Organise and Collective Bargaining Convention, 1949 (No. 98), which remain the two most important ILO Conventions in the field of trade union rights.

Since their adoption, Conventions Nos. 87 and 98 have been reinforced by several other instruments adopted by the International Labour Conference concerning trade union rights and various aspects of labour-management relations. The Consultation (Industrial and National Levels) Recommendation, 1960 (No. 113), urges appropriate measures to promote effective consultation and co-operation between public authorities and employers' and workers' organisations with a view to developing the economy as a whole or individual branches of it, improving conditions of work and raising standards of living. In 1971 a Convention (No. 135) and a Recommendation (No. 143) were adopted concerning the protection and facilities to be afforded to workers' representatives in enterprises: these texts are intended to protect workers' representatives against action taken against them because of their activities in that capacity or because of their union membership, and to ensure that workers' representatives in enterprises are afforded appropriate facilities to enable them to carry out their functions promptly and efficiently. In 1975 the Rural Workers' Organisations Convention (No. 141) and Recommendation (No. 149) were adopted; the Convention commits ratifying States to facilitating the establishment and growth on a voluntary basis of strong and independent organisations of workers as an effective means of ensuring the participation of rural workers in economic and social development and in the benefits resulting from such development. The Tripartite Consultation (International Labour Standards) Convention, 1976 (No. 144), to which repeated references were made in Chapter 5, emphasises that the workers' and employers' organisations taking part in the consultations in question are to enjoy freedom of association. The Labour Relations (Public Service) Convention (No. 151) and Recommendation (No. 159), adopted in 1978, aim at protecting the right of public employees to organise and promoting their participation in the determination of their conditions of employment. The last instruments adopted by the Conference in the labour relations field are the Collective Bargaining Convention (No. 154) and Recommendation (No. 163), of 1981, which seek to promote the development of collective bargaining.

Mention should also be made here of a resolution concerning trade union rights and their relation to civil liberties, adopted by the International Labour Conference in 1970. The resolution lists the civil liberties that are essential for the normal exercise of trade union rights, namely the right to freedom and security of person and freedom from arbitrary arrest and detention, freedom of opinion and expression;

freedom of assembly; the right to a fair trial by an independent and impartial tribunal; and the right to protection of the property of trade union organisations. In 1987 the International Labour Conference adopted a resolution concerning the 40th anniversary of the adoption of the Freedom of Association and Protection of the Right to Organise Convention, 1948 (No. 87). The resolution urges the member States which have not yet ratified this Convention to do their utmost to ratify it in the course of 1988. Furthermore, it calls upon the governments of all member States to take all necessary steps for the full implementation of the Convention.

The vital importance attached by the ILO to the observance of the principles and guarantees of freedom of association has led to the establishment of special procedures for the examination of complaints regarding infringements of trade union rights. In the remainder of the present chapter we shall be looking at the origins, the functioning and the results of these procedures. First, however, two points deserve to be borne in mind. The first is that the special freedom of association procedures supplement but are not substitutes for either the regular, routine supervisory procedures described in Chapter 6 or the special procedures for representations and complaints which we examined in Chapter 7. The second is that the procedures we are about to examine can be brought into play against governments even if they have not ratified the ILO's freedom of association Conventions. This latter aspect of the procedures deserves some explanation: why is it regarded as proper to allow complaints proceedings to be conducted regarding the non-compliance by governments with principles laid down in Conventions which they have not ratified, i.e. in respect of which they have assumed no formal obligations?

To begin with, it deserves to be pointed out that the ILO's special freedom of association machinery was established – on the basis of a formal agreement between the ILO and the Economic and Social Council of the United Nations – as far back as in 1950, i.e. at a point in time at which it was not known to what extent the Conventions on freedom of association adopted in the previous two years would in fact be ratified by member States and thus be embraced by the regular ILO supervisory procedures with regard to ratified ILO Conventions. A need was therefore felt for machinery that could operate even in the absence of ratification. Moreover, membership of the ILO is conditional upon the formal acceptance of the obligations of the ILO Constitution which, as we saw earlier, affirms the principle of freedom of association: in 1995 the Fourth European Regional Conference of the ILO reiterated that it was one of the objectives embodied in the ILO Constitution and should accordingly be observed by member States by reason of their membership of the Organisation.

The machinery established as a result of the above-mentioned ILO-United Nations agreement comprises two bodies: the Fact-Finding and Conciliation Commission on Freedom of Association and the Governing Body Committee on Freedom of Association.

The Fact-Finding and Conciliation Commission

The Fact-Finding and Conciliation Commission on Freedom of Association was established in 1950. The members are highly qualified, independent persons appointed by the ILO Governing Body for the purpose of examining complaints concerning alleged infringements of trade union rights. In exercising these functions, the Commission generally works in panels composed of three members. It is essentially a fact-finding body, but is also authorised to discuss the problems referred to it for investigation with the government concerned, with a view to securing an agreed solution to those problems. Only a complaint submitted by a government or by an employers' or workers' organisation is receivable; the organisation must be a national one with a direct interest in the matter, an international one having consultative status with the ILO, or some other international employers' or workers' organisation if the allegations relate to matters directly affecting its affiliated organisations. Special arrangements have been agreed upon between the Economic and Social Council of the United Nations and the ILO Governing Body concerning allegations received by the United Nations regarding infringements of trade union rights. If complaints against ILO member States are received by the United Nations, they are forwarded by the Economic and Social Council to the ILO, and the Governing Body then considers the question of their referral to the Fact-Finding and Conciliation Commission. If the United Nations or the ILO receives a complaint against a country that is a member of the United Nations but not a Member of the ILO, it is for the Economic and Social Council to decide what action to take in the matter, either by seeking the consent of the government concerned to the referral of the case to the Commission or in any other manner.

This brings us to an interesting procedural aspect of the functions of the Fact-Finding and Conciliation Commission, namely the fact that in principle no case can be submitted to the Commission for investigation unless the government concerned has agreed. An exception to this rule can be made only if the government has ratified the relevant freedom of association Conventions, in which case the Commission can be designated as a commission of inquiry under article 26 of the ILO Constitution. For a number of years the necessity of obtaining the consent of the government concerned before a case could be investigated by the Fact-Finding and Conciliation Commission severely crippled the whole procedure. The first government to give its consent to the Commission was Japan in 1964. Subsequently, a further five cases have been examined by the Commission. These have related to Greece (1965-66), Lesotho (1973-75), Chile (1974-75), the United States (Puerto Rico, 1979-81), and South Africa (1991). The case of Chile provides a good example of how the Commission performs its functions:

In October 1974 the Commission held a session in Geneva, during which it heard the witnesses proposed by the principal complainant organisations (the three major organisations of workers) and by the Government. In November-December 1974 it visited Chile, having first made appropriate arrangements to ensure that the necessary facilities would be accorded (e.g. to meet freely, and without the presence of witnesses, any person who might wish to be heard by the Commission, and a guarantee that any persons so heard would not, in any circumstances, be penalised as a result). In Chile the Commission went to various regions and visited a number of enterprises. It interviewed the authorities, various personalities, a large number of trade union leaders (some of whom were in detention), employers and employers' representatives and workers who had been dismissed, as well as professors, lawyers and members of the clergy. Before it left Chile, the Commission informed the Government of some preliminary conclusions it had reached and made certain recommendations. The Commission's final report was drawn up in April-May 1975; it dealt not only with trade union questions but also with human rights and civil liberties, which have a direct bearing on the effective exercise of trade union rights. In the Governing Body in May 1975, the representative of the Government of Chile, while making certain observations on the report, stated that his Government accepted the Commission's recommendations. The Governing Body urged the Government to give effect to them, and has repeatedly asked the Government to report in detail on the measures taken to apply them; the reports are examined by the Governing Body Committee on Freedom of Association and by the Governing Body itself.

The Governing Body Committee

The decision to set up a Committee on Freedom of Association was taken by the Governing Body in 1951. At that initial stage, the Committee was merely required to carry out a preliminary examination, with a view to determining whether a complaint was sufficiently well founded to warrant its submission to the Fact-Finding and Conciliation Commission. In practice, however, things were to turn out quite differently: because it was difficult to bring cases before the Commission, the Committee quickly developed into a body that examines the substance of the case before it, and submits its findings to the Governing Body.

Apart from an independent chairman the Committee has nine members, three each from the Government, Workers' and Employers' groups of the Governing Body. It meets three times a year; its functions are of a quasi-judicial nature and the procedure it follows conforms to the basic principles that apply to proceedings in a court of law. Complaints must be submitted either by workers' or employers' organisations or by governments, and may, it will be recalled, be made even against a government that has not ratified the freedom of association Conventions. When a complaint is received, it is communicated to the government concerned for its observations, while the complaining organisation is allowed a specified period in which to supply further information, which is also communicated to the government. In certain cases the Committee may decide that the substance of a government's reply is to be communicated to the complainants for comments, to which the government will subsequently be given the opportunity to reply in turn. If a government delays in forwarding its observations, the Committee makes a special appeal to it and subsequently the reasons for the delay in transmitting the observations may be discussed by the Chairman of the Committee with the government's representatives attending the International Labour Conference. If certain governments persistently fail to reply, the Committee submits a report on the substance of the case, and wider publicity is then given to the allegations, the decisions of the Governing Body and the obstructive attitude of the government. In practice, however, it is seldom necessary to have recourse to such action.

Once in possession of all this evidence, the Committee examines the arguments of the parties and formulates its conclusions, which may consist in the dismissal of a complaint, in its entirety or in part, or in a statement to the effect that a case of infringement has been made out, in which case it draws the attention of the government concerned to the principles and standards in relation to freedom of association that have been infringed, and recommends the steps that should be taken to remedy the situation. The decisions of the Committee are adopted unanimously.

Prior to this the Committee, or in particularly urgent or serious cases the Director-General with the approval of the Chairman of the Committee, may request the government concerned to allow a representative of the Director-General to carry out an inquiry on the spot into the matters involved in the complaint, with a view to drawing up a report on the facts on which the Committee can subsequently base its conclusions or recommendations. This "direct contacts" procedure, which has been successfully used in several cases, is very similar to the procedure described earlier in Chapter 6.

When the Committee on Freedom of Association has reached its conclusions on a complaint, this does not necessarily mean that the matter is closed. If an infringement of trade union rights has been established, the government concerned may be asked by the Governing Body to take remedial action and to report back within a specific time on the action that has been taken. Moreover, if it is necessary to remedy a situation in which freedom of association is being infringed, and if the government has ratified the freedom of association Conventions in question, the matter is referred to the Committee of Experts on the Application of Conventions and Recommendations, so that it may be followed up under the regular supervision procedure.

The Committee, established in 1951, has dealt with over 1,800 cases, covering an enormous variety of factual and legal situations, and has pronounced on allegations of infringements of trade union rights in every part of the world and every type of society. Subjects that have frequently been brought before the Committee for examination include all aspects of the setting up of organisations and the right to join them, election to and removal from trade union office, non-interference with trade union administration and activities, dissolution or suspension of organisations, acts of anti-union discrimination in employment, the right to collective bargaining, the right to strike, arrests of trade unionists, and the prohibition of trade union meetings and demonstrations. It would take up too much space to examine the principles developed by the Committee with regard to all of these questions. Let us none the less take a closer look at three selected issues, partly because they are important and partly because they are among the ones that crop up most frequently in public debate: the right to strike, union security arrangements in the form of closed-shop and similar clauses, and the relationship between trade union rights and civil liberties.

The right to strike

Contrary to what people sometimes appear to believe, there is no provision in any international labour Convention or Recommendation specifically recognising the right to strike or defining the extent to which it may be exercised. Cases relating to the right to strike are none the less among those that come before the Committee most frequently. In such cases, the Committee has pointed out that the right to strike is one of the essential means by which workers and their organisations can promote and defend their occupational interests, that the right is generally recognised and that allegations relating to it are not outside the Committee's competence in so far as they concern the exercise of trade union rights.

While upholding the principle of the right to strike, the Committee has agreed that it is permissible for certain temporary restrictions to be placed upon the exercise of that right.

The right to strike can be subject to restrictions or prohibitions for public servants engaged in the administration of the State and for workers providing essential services in the strictest sense. This refers to "services the interruption of which would endanger the life, personal safety or health of the whole or part of the population". The fire service, for example, could be deemed an essential service in the strict sense. This notion largely depends upon the specific conditions of each country.

There can, however, be an expansion of the scope of application of restrictions or prohibitions in the case of a strike the extent and duration of which might be such as to endanger the normal living conditions of the population, or in the event of an acute national crisis (insurrection, natural disaster, etc.), and for a limited period, or if the circumstances justify that an inessential service be considered an essential one, in a strict sense. A good example would be maritime transport, the interruption of which would make life difficult for the inhabitants of islands. A minimum service could be established in such a case.

The restriction could be the need to give advance warning of a strike to the authorities, or to exhaust all the negotiating, conciliation and arbitration procedures before starting strike action. Strikes could also be banned if they constitute a violation of a collective agreement.

Nevertheless, the above-mentioned restrictions or prohibitions must be accompanied by adequate guarantees to safeguard the workers' interests. These should include appropriate, impartial and speedy conciliation and arbitration procedures, in which the parties can participate at each stage; judgements and awards should have the same obligatory force for each side and be implemented rapidly.

Restrictions on the right to strike in certain occupations or services, to the extent necessary to comply with statutory safety requirements, have also been held to be normal by the Committee.

On the other hand, where legislation – in normal times – has directly or indirectly placed a ban on strikes in all spheres of activity, the Committee has stated that such a ban may constitute an important restriction of the potential activities of trade unions, and would therefore not be in conformity with the generally recognised principles of freedom of association.

When strikes happen, the Committee on Freedom of Association has indicated that the replacement of striking workers during a legal strike would be contrary to the right to strike and would constitute a violation of trade union rights.

As for sanctions taken in the case of legal strikes, it would be a violation of freedom of association with grave risks of abuse if extremely serious measures were to be taken, such as redundancy and refusal to rehire strikers because of their participation in the strike.

Union security arrangements

As regards the closed shop, the union shop and preferential employment of trade union members, it should be mentioned that at the time of the adoption of Convention No. 98, it was made clear by the International Labour Conference that the Convention should not be interpreted either as authorising or as prohibiting such union security arrangements, which were to be governed by national practice. This clarification is of particular importance for countries with more than one trade union movement. It follows from the principle laid down by the Conference that no State is in any way bound by the Convention to recognise or to tolerate union security clauses; but that if in a given country such clauses are acceptable under the law or admitted in practice, then there is nothing to prevent that country from ratifying and applying the Convention. It is on these grounds that the Committee on Freedom of Association has always declined to examine allegations or complaints relating to the existence of union security measures.

Trade union rights and civil liberties

Time and again, the Committee has stressed the importance it attaches to respect for various civil liberties in connection with the complaints that have come before it, and has stated in more general terms that a genuinely free and independent trade union movement can develop only under a regime that guarantees fundamental human rights. The Committee has been guided in reaching its conclusions by the basic principles on the subjects as set out, in particular, in the Universal Declaration of Human Rights. The International Labour Conference has placed the full weight of its authority behind the Committee's findings by adopting in 1970 the resolution concerning trade union rights and their relation to civil liberties, which as we saw earlier in this chapter enumerates the civil liberties that are considered essential for the normal exercise of trade union rights.

To take just one of these basic liberties, the Committee has often been confronted with allegations concerning the arrest of trade unionists. Here the Committee has always considered that it falls upon the governments concerned to furnish proof that the arrest had no connection with trade union activities. On many occasions, when governments have replied to allegations that trade union leaders or workers have been arrested for trade union activities by stating that the persons in question were in reality arrested for subversive activities, for reasons of internal security or for ordinary crimes, the Committee has followed the rule that the governments concerned should be requested to provide more precise information concerning the arrests and the exact grounds for them, including the full texts of any judgements. In the same connection, the Committee has emphasised the importance it attaches to the principle of prompt and fair trial by an independent and impartial judiciary in every case. In certain cases, because it had received information from the governments concerned showing sufficiently clearly and precisely that the arrests were due to activities outside the trade union sphere that were either prejudicial to public order or of a political nature, the Committee has reached the conclusion that the allegations did not call for further examination.

Results achieved

To what extent is it possible to measure the results achieved by the Committee on Freedom of Association over the years? How effective is all this? In a number of cases, particularly those connected with a difficult political situation, the results have been disappointing, and both trade union rights and civil liberties have continued to be violated in the countries concerned, regardless of any recommendations made by the Committee. In a great many cases, however, tangible and positive results have been achieved. Thus, it is known that in many instances, as a result of recommendations made by the Committee, legislation criticised has been repealed or amended, practices incompatible with the principle of freedom of association have been discontinued, situations giving rise to complaints have been remedied, imprisoned trade union leaders have been released, and in some cases death sentences on trade unionists have been commuted. Other results are less tangible but equally important. The Worker members of the Governing Body are well aware of the various difficulties and make constant efforts to improve the procedure. On the other hand, experience has, for instance, shown that the mere possibility of recourse to the complaints procedure has sometimes led the parties concerned to remedy an existing situation merely in order to avoid having it investigated at the international level. In other cases, the fact that a complaint has been lodged has acted as a spur to negotiations between the government and the trade union concerned, and has finally led to a settlement and a withdrawal of the complaint. There may also be cases in which a government refrains from taking certain measures affecting freedom of association because of the possibility that the Committee might be asked to intervene. Thus, the mere existence of the Committee on Freedom of Association may well have prevented at least as many injustices as those which it has had to consider.

Perhaps, in the final analysis, the greatest achievement of the Committee lies in its success in gaining recognition for the international validity of the principles of freedom of association, and in establishing a measure of international accountability by governments for their trade union policies. Through its success in these respects, the Committee has certainly made a very important contribution to the promotion of one of the most fundamental human rights.

Points for discussion

1. Describe the content of ILO standards in the field of trade union rights.
2. What is the scope of protection provided for by the ILO's supervisory system in the field of trade union rights? Is it limited only to the text of the relevant ILO Conventions?
3. Describe the procedure of the Governing Body Committee on Freedom of Association.
4. Which Conventions in the field of trade union rights has your country ratified, and which Recommendations has it accepted?
5. If your Government has not ratified the two basic Conventions in this field (Nos. 87 and 98), find out the reasons given by the Government for not having done so. What has been the reaction of your trade union organisation to this?
6. What is your opinion on the effectiveness of the ILO's procedures in the field of the protection of trade union rights?

Group exercise

Try to formulate the text of a complaint concerning the violation of trade union rights, having regard to all the possibilities of trade unions in the procedure for examination of the complaint by the Committee on Freedom of Association.

Further reading

ILO: *Trade union participation in the ILO supervisory system for the protection of trade union rights*, course topic, Geneva, 1994, available from the Bureau of Workers' Activities.

ILO: *Freedom of association: Digest of decisions and principles of the Freedom of Association Committee of the Governing Body of the ILO*, fourth edition, Geneva, 1996.

ILO: *Human rights – A common responsibility*, Report of the Director-General (Part 1), International Labour Conference, 75th Session, 1988, Geneva, 1988.

ILO: *Freedom of association,* a workers' education manual, second (revised) edition, Geneva, 1987.

ILO: *ILO law on freedom of association: Standards and procedures*, Geneva, 1995.

Chapter 9

Influence of international labour standards

The value of Conventions and Recommendations depends largely on the action taken to make them effective at the national level. But how can we know how much influence the standards incorporated in these Conventions and Recommendations may have over the years on social legislation around the world? It is certainly difficult to measure this influence with any degree of certainty, since a great many factors usually contribute to the introduction of any given social measure. However, a number of studies have been written on the impact of international labour standards in general or in various countries (see the bibliography), and this chapter will give some indication of the different ways in which these standards have contributed to improvements in national legislation and practice.

The general influence of ILO standards on national legislation is widely recognised and has frequently been referred to by governments. It is clear, from examples in many countries, that the texts of the relevant Conventions and Recommendations are consulted in the stage of preparation of new labour legislation.

Action taken as a consequence of submission to the competent authorities

We have seen above (Chapter 5) that all Conventions and Recommendations must be submitted to the national parliament or other competent authority, soon after adoption by the ILO. The examination of the provisions laid down in the new Convention or Recommendation and the comparison between these and the national provisions – which is normally made by the government in this connection – often leads the government to introduce new social measures. This may be merely with a view to bringing the national legislation into line with internationally adopted standards, or may be the first step towards ratification and formal acceptance. The influence of this procedure has been demonstrated by many ratifications, following the submission of newly adopted ILO instruments.

Effect of ratification

In many countries the significance of ratification has been considerable; in some it may have an immediate effect on national legislation because of the State's constitutional system or special provisions of ratification laws. A few historical cases may illustrate this better. For example, a study carried out in 1958 showed that most of the Conventions ratified by Switzerland had a marked effect on the federal legislation; in Norway it has been stated that of the 57 Conventions which that country had ratified by 1964, well over half had directly influenced the legislation and practice existing at the time of ratification; and in Poland it was estimated in 1965 that 34 of the 51 ratified Conventions had had some influence on the country's legislation and that in 17 cases influence had been significant and often decisive.

This influence of ratified Conventions may make itself felt in various ways and at different procedural stages. We have already seen that the submission of Conventions to the parliament or other competent authority may lead to improved application and to ratification. However, independently of this formal procedure, a government may decide that the time has come to ratify a Convention, and may enact new legislation to meet its requirements. As far back as 1925 the British Parliament passed the Merchant Shipping (International Labour Conventions) Act for the express purpose of giving effect to three maritime Conventions and permitting their ratification.

In Iraq a 1973 amendment to the Labour Law provisions on holidays with pay contained a statement of reasons for the Government's decision to ratify the Holidays with Pay Convention (Revised), 1970 (No. 132), and to introduce the necessary amendment into the Labour Law. In Zambia the ratification of the Medical Examination of Young Persons (Underground Work) Convention, 1965 (No. 124), was preceded by an "Act to provide for the implementation in Zambia of the International Labour Organisation's Convention No. 124", the text of which was reproduced in a schedule to the Act. The main purpose of the adoption in Belgium in 1965 of a law relating to the protection of wages was to permit the ratification of the Protection of Wages Convention, 1949 (No. 95). In 1969 the Government of Cameroon issued two orders governing the work of women and young persons which made possible the ratification of ten Conventions in the following year (Nos. 3, 5, 10, 15, 16, 77, 78, 89, 90 and 123). In the Federal Republic of Germany the adoption of the Employment Policy Convention, 1964 (No. 122), contributed to the preparation of a detailed employment and economic programme and the enactment of a new body of laws on employment policy in 1969, thus paving the way for the ratification of the Convention in 1971.

In some countries, legislative amendments which are necessary to give effect to a Convention are introduced by the very Act which authorises ratification. In Costa Rica, for example, the 1960 Act of ratification of the two freedom of association Conventions (Nos. 87 and 98) contained provisions amending the Labour Code so as to eliminate the possibility of dissolving trade unions by administrative decision and authorise the affiliation of federations of employers and workers with international employers' or workers' organisations. Ratification sometimes also has an immediate effect on national legislation because under the constitutional system of certain countries or special provisions of ratification laws, ratified Conventions automatically become part of the law of the land and are therefore directly enforceable by the courts. This is the position in France, for example, where the courts decided that certain provisions of the Maternity Convention, 1919 (No. 3), prevailed over conflicting legislation; and in Madagascar, where the Supreme Court decided in 1969 that the Freedom of Association and Protection of the Right to Organise Convention, 1948 (No. 87), had been incorporated in the national legislation as a result of ratification.

In some cases, even if no reference is made to a ratified Convention in the relevant legislation, its influence is demonstrated by the fact that its essential provisions are reproduced word for word in national legislation. Thus more than a score of countries have included in their legislation various clauses of the Labour Inspection Convention, 1947 (No. 81), and the definition of forced labour contained in Convention No. 29, of 1930, can be found in the legislation of several African countries.

Effect of supervision

Measures such as those indicated above are usually taken on a national initiative. However, it is often at the request of the ILO supervisory bodies that the government introduces measures to ensure fuller conformity with ratified Conventions, and each year a whole series of cases is recorded by the ILO's Committee of Experts. The essential purpose of the supervisory system is to ensure that freely assumed obligations are honoured, and thus to maintain the credibility of the act of ratification. The ILO supervisory procedures can also assist member States to understand the full import of the standards which they have undertaken to observe and prompt them to make good any shortcomings in meeting those requirements. Progress in this respect, following comments and recommendations by the Committee of Experts, is often facilitated and speeded up through direct contacts between representatives of the Director-General and the governments concerned, in the course of which misunderstandings may be cleared up and any necessary amending legislation drafted, or through more informal assistance by the ILO. In other cases the effect of supervision is reflected in a succession of steps taken by the national authorities over a long period. This occurs particularly with promotional Conventions such as those dealing with employment policy, discrimination in employment, or the protection of indigenous peoples, where full application is necessarily a long-term process. However, it should be noted that the impact of the ILO supervisory procedures is not only confined to cases where critical comments after ratification lead to remedial measures. These procedures also exert a significant indirect influence which is preventive in nature.

Stimulation through reporting on unratified Conventions and on Recommendations

Each year, as we saw in Chapter 5, governments must report to the ILO on selected Recommendations, or on selected Conventions that have not been ratified, indicating what difficulties have been encountered in giving effect to the Recommendation or Convention in question. These reports may lead to the adoption of new measures in three ways. To begin with the government itself, when it examines the national provisions on the subject, may find that the time has come to bring its legislation up to the level of the international standards, and possibly to ratify the Convention. Secondly, the Committee of Experts is often in a position to indicate or suggest useful means of overcoming obstacles reported by governments as hindering full compliance with the Convention or Recommendation. Thirdly, the tripartite Conference committee on the application of Conventions and Recommendations, when it discusses these reviews each year, sometimes appeals to the governments concerned to take any necessary action, and these appeals can produce results, particularly when backed up by national workers' or employers' organisations that have been represented on the Conference committee.

Effectiveness of international labour standards regardless of obligations

A Convention or Recommendation often has a significant influence on national law and practice quite independently of any obligations under ILO procedures and even if the Convention has not been ratified: again and again, it is found that the provisions embodied in these texts are used as source material when national laws are being prepared.

Thus, Conventions relating to the protection of seafarers have left their imprint on the legislation and practice of many maritime countries, and in Tunisia for example the Maritime Labour Code promulgated in 1967 was based largely on international labour standards. In another field, that of holidays with pay, a review carried out in 1984 noted that in more than 60 countries legislation had been inspired by the respective Conventions, most particularly by the Holidays with Pay Convention (Revised), 1970 (No. 132), as regards the minimum length of basic holiday (three working weeks for one year of service).

In the case of equal remuneration, a review made in 1986 pointed out that while the Equal Remuneration Convention, 1951 (No. 100), which is one of the ILO instruments having received the greatest number of ratifications, had only been ratified by slightly over two-thirds of the member States, it had played and continued to play, together with the accompanying Recommendation (No. 90), an essential role in the promotion of equality all over the world. Convention No. 100 has now been ratified by over three-quarters of the member States. The two equal pay instruments have been the basis for an undeniably just claim by the workers, and they have thus contributed to a greater acceptance of the principle that there must be no discrimination between women and men in remuneration for work of equal value.

Recommendations may also have much influence on national legislation. For example, since the adoption in 1963 of the Termination of Employment Recommendation (No. 119), its provisions have been reflected in the legislation both of highly industrialised countries such as France, Sweden and the United Kingdom and in developing countries such as Colombia, Cyprus, Mauritius, Panama, the United Republic of Tanzania and Zaire. A multitude of examples such as these may be found to illustrate the spontaneous effect which ILO standards have in all the fields they cover.

In certain cases, where the provisions of international labour standards are reflected neither in the laws of the country nor in collective agreements, they may nevertheless have a real impact at the national level. This occurs for example in countries (including Colombia, Costa Rica and Honduras) where the Labour Code lays down the general principle that cases not covered by any specific legislative provision shall be determined by reference to ILO, among other things, Conventions (whether ratified or not) and Recommendations. It also occurs when ILO standards are relied upon by courts of law in interpreting constitutional guarantees of social rights; this has been the case, for instance, in Trinidad and Tobago as regards the Freedom of Association and Protection of the Right to Organise Convention, 1948 (No. 87), and in Italy as regards Recommendation No. 119.

The initiative for incorporating international labour standards in national legislation usually comes from the governments themselves. Sometimes, however, such measures are taken on the advice of ILO technical co-operation experts who are called in by the government to help draft laws: in the past decade nearly 100 countries have had recourse to ILO assistance in the preparation of labour laws, either general labour codes or legislation on specific questions such as social security; over 40 countries have had assistance from the ILO in drawing up legislation in this field alone, and in most of these countries it has led to the improved application of the relevant ILO Conventions and Recommendations.

There are other cases, however, in which the government concerned may hesitate to introduce new measures corresponding to international labour standards and where it is the workers' organisations that take the initiative and see to it that the international legislation is brought up to the level fixed in Conventions and Recommendations. In Japan, for example, the trade unions have carried out various campaigns to secure the implementation of ILO standards with regard to freedom of association and machinery for the determination of minimum wages; after these campaigns the national laws were changed and ultimately the Conventions in question were ratified. These trade unions also campaigned for legislative changes to make possible the application of the ILO Conventions relating to night work of women, maternity protection and discrimination in employment. Similarly in the United Kingdom, the equal remuneration Convention and Recommendation, 1951, provided backing for a trade union campaign to secure the implementation of the principle of equal pay for work of equal value, which led to the enactment of new legislation and the ratification of the Convention.

In yet other cases the initiative for introducing new legislation patterned on ILO standards is taken by tripartite labour advisory bodies. These can be particularly effective when they carry out periodic or ad hoc reviews of unratified Conventions and of Recommendations in order to ascertain whether measures should not be introduced to put them into effect. Many countries have already established such a system. In Australia, for example, in 1968, the tripartite National Labour Advisory Council undertook a comprehensive review of the country's position in relation to all ILO Conventions, and that review led to the ratification of six Conventions. In Canada a unit in the Federal Labour Department prepares comparative studies each year on selected unratified Conventions and Canadian laws and practice; the studies are circulated for comment to the provincial governments, and to workers' and employers' organisations. In India the tripartite Committee on Conventions periodically reviews selected Conventions and Recommendations and proposes measures for their progressive application and eventual ratification.

The influence of such tripartite procedures in promoting the acceptance of ILO standards should increase following the adoption, in 1976, of Convention No. 144 and Recommendation No. 152 concerning tripartite consultations. The aim of these texts is to ensure full involvement of both workers' and employers' organisations in ILO standard-setting activities, from the time when draft standards are first considered until they are applied at the national level. These procedures are now in use in many countries, and contribute to the wider application of Conventions and Recommendations, as well as giving trade unionists in many countries more opportunity to press for fuller application of international labour standards.

So far, we have seen mainly examples of the influence of Conventions and Recommendations on national legislation. But in many countries these standards are also freely quoted in collective bargaining, since union negotiators find that they are in a stronger position if they can back their claims with an international standard adopted at the ILO Conference. In this connection the General Secretary of the International Federation of Commercial, Clerical and Technical Employees stated in 1969 that even when ILO standards "are not included in the legislative codes of member States, they nevertheless serve as a yardstick in the negotiations between labour and management everywhere, especially as regards the successful conclusion of collective agreements". Specific examples may be found in many countries, including the Federal Republic of Germany, where a collective agreement on works medical services, and particularly the supplementary guide-lines issued in 1966, were largely inspired by the ILO's Recommendation of 1959 on occupational health services; in Kenya, where the Industrial Relations Charter agreed upon by the Government and the central employers' and workers' organisations in 1962 provided for observation by management and by the unions of the Right to Organise and Collective Bargaining Convention, 1949 (No. 98), and for the implementation of Article 14 of the Social Policy (Basic Means and Standards) Convention, 1962 (No. 117), relating to the elimination of discrimination in employment on grounds of race, colour, sex, belief, tribal association or trade union affiliation; in Poland, where the Hours of Work (Coal Mines) Convention, 1935 (No. 46), was implemented by a collective agreement in 1957; and in the United Kingdom where, according to a government spokesman, the ILO's maritime Convention on wages, hours of work and manning has exerted immense influence on collective bargaining.

Conclusion

This concludes our brief survey of the practical effect of the ILO's standard-setting work. Much more could have been said on the subject, but a number of examples chosen more or less at random have had to suffice. These examples have none the less served to illustrate at least three important points.

The first is that international labour standards have exerted and continue to exert their influence in every corner of the world, in industrialised and developing countries alike, and that the policy constantly pursued by the ILO of adopting standards designed to be universally applicable would appear to be still fully valid today.

The second is that this sizeable effect in all the member countries of the ILO has been due in no small measure to the efficacy of the procedures, constitutional and other, for promoting and supervising the application of ILO standards, as described in this manual.

The third is that, in many instances, action in member States to secure the application of ILO standards has been prompted by workers and their organisations, acting either on their own or through tripartite advisory bodies. It is to be hoped that this book will succeed in giving workers and others – who are interested in but not yet familiar with the ILO and its standards – a reasonably full understanding of the different stages of the standard-setting process and the ensuing supervisory procedures. To the extent that it does succeed, it will strengthen the hands of all who see in international labour standards an important means of promoting human rights and social justice.

Points for discussion

1. What do you think is the effect of international labour standards on labour legislation in your country?
2. Give examples of newly adopted national laws or regulations inspired by the content of the relevant ILO Conventions and Recommendations, even in the absence of ratification.
3. Give examples of remedial changes in national legislation in response to comments by the Committee of Experts on the Application of Conventions and Recommendations.
4. How does your trade union organisation contribute to incorporating the requirements of international labour standards into the national legislation of your country?

Further reading

ILO: *The ILO, standard setting and globalization*, Report of the Director-General, International Labour Conference, 85th Session (Geneva), 1997.

ILO: *The impact of international labour Conventions and Recommendations*, Geneva, 1996.

Appendix 1

Classified guide to international labour standards

(Including instruments adopted up to the
85th Session of the International Labour Conference, 1997)

I. Basic human rights

A. *Freedom of association*

Freedom of Association and Protection of the Right to Organise Convention, 1948 (No. 87).

Right to Organise and Collective Bargaining Convention, 1949 (No. 98).

Workers' Representatives Convention (No. 135) and Recommendation (No. 143), 1971.

Rural Workers' Organisations Convention (No. 141) and Recommendation (No. 149), 1975.

Labour Relations (Public Service) Convention (No. 151) and Recommendation (No. 159), 1978.

Right of Association (Agriculture) Convention, 1921 (No. 11).

Right of Association (Non-Metropolitan Territories) Convention, 1947 (No. 84).

B. *Forced labour*

Forced Labour Convention, 1930 (No. 29).

Forced Labour (Indirect Compulsion) Recommendation, 1930 (No. 35).

Abolition of Forced Labour Convention, 1956 (No. 105).

C. *Equality of opportunity and treatment*

Equal Remuneration Convention (No. 100) and Recommendation (No. 90), 1951.

Discrimination (Employment and Occupation) Convention (No. 111) and Recommendation (No. 111), 1958.

Workers with Family Responsibilities Convention (No. 156) and Recommendation (No. 165), 1981.

II. Employment

A. *Employment policy*

Unemployment Convention, 1919 (No. 2).

Employment Policy Convention (No. 122) and Recommendation (No. 122), 1964.

Special Youth Schemes Recommendation, 1970 (No. 136).

Employment Policy (Supplementary Provisions) Recommendation, 1984 (No. 169).

Employment Promotion and Protection against Unemployment Convention (No. 168) and Recommendation (No. 176), 1988.

B. *Employment services and fee-charging employment agencies*

Employment Service Convention (No. 88) and Recommendation (No. 83), 1948.

Fee-Charging Employment Agencies Convention, 1933 (No. 34).

Fee-Charging Employment Agencies Convention (Revised), 1949 (No. 96).

Private Employment Agencies Convention (No. 181) and Recommendation (No. 188), 1997.

C. *Vocational guidance and training*

Human Resources Development Convention (No. 142) and Recommendation (No. 150), 1975.

D. *Rehabilitation and employment of disabled persons*

Vocational Rehabilitation (Disabled) Recommendation, 1955 (No. 99).

Vocational Rehabilitation and Employment (Disabled Persons) Convention (No. 159) and Recommendation (No. 168), 1983.

E. *Employment security*

Termination of Employment Convention (No. 158) and Recommendation (No. 166), 1982.

III. Social policy

Social Policy (Non-Metropolitan Territories) Convention, 1947 (No. 82).

Social Policy (Basic Aims and Standards) Convention, 1962 (No. 117).

Co-operatives (Developing Countries) Recommendation, 1966 (No. 127).

IV. Labour administration

A. *General*

Labour Administration Convention (No. 150) and Recommendation (No. 158), 1978.

B. *Labour inspection*

Labour Inspection Convention (No. 81) and Recommendation (No. 81), 1947 [and Protocol, 1995].

Labour Inspectorates (Non-Metropolitan Territories) Convention, 1947 (No. 85).

Labour Inspection (Mining and Transport) Recommendation, 1947 (No. 82).

Labour Inspection (Agriculture) Convention (No. 129) and Recommendation (No. 133), 1969.

C. *Employment service and fee-charging employment agencies*

See II.B above.

D. *Statistics*

Labour Statistics Convention (No. 160) and Recommendation (No. 170), 1985.

E. *Tripartite consultation*

Tripartite Consultation (International Labour Standards) Convention, 1976 (No. 144).

Tripartite Consultation (Activities of the International Labour Organisation) Recommendation, 1976 (No. 152).

V. Industrial relations

See I.A above.

Collective Agreements Recommendation, 1951 (No. 91).

Collective Bargaining Convention (No. 154) and Recommendation (No. 163), 1981.

Voluntary Conciliation and Arbitration Recommendation, 1951 (No. 92).

Co-operation at the Level of the Undertaking Recommendation, 1952 (No. 94).

Consultation (Industrial and National Levels) Recommendation, 1960 (No. 113).

Communications within the Undertaking Recommendation, 1967 (No. 129).

Examination of Grievances Recommendation, 1967 (No. 130).

VI. Conditions of work

A. *Wages*

1. *Minimum Wage-Fixing Machinery*

Minimum Wage-Fixing Machinery Convention, 1928 (No. 26).

Minimum Wage-Fixing Machinery (Agriculture) Convention, 1951 (No. 99).

Minimum Wage-Fixing Convention (No. 131) and Recommendation (No. 135), 1970.

2. *Protection of wages*

Protection of Wages Convention (No. 95) and Recommendation (No. 85), 1949.

Protection of Workers' Claims (Employer's Insolvency) Convention (No. 173) and Recommendation (No. 180), 1992.

3. *Labour clauses in public contracts*

Labour Clauses (Public Contracts) Convention (No. 94) and Recommendation (No. 84), 1949.

B. *General conditions of employment*

1. *Hours of work*

Hours of Work (Industry) Convention, 1919 (No. 1).

Hours of Work (Commerce and Offices) Convention, 1930 (No. 30).

Forty-Hour Week Convention, 1935 (No. 47).

Reduction of Hours of Work Recommendation, 1962 (No. 116).

Sheet-Glass Works Convention, 1934 (No. 43).

Reduction of Hours of Work (Glass-Bottle Works) Convention, 1935 (No. 49).

Hours of Work and Rest Periods (Road Transport) Convention, 1939 (No. 67).

Hours of Work and Rest Periods (Road Transport) Convention (No. 153) and Recommendation (No. 161), 1979.

Part-Time Work Convention (No. 175) and Recommendation (No. 182), 1994.

2. *Night work*

Night Work (Bakeries) Convention, 1925 (No. 20).

3. *Weekly rest*

Weekly Rest (Industry) Convention, 1921 (No. 14).

Weekly Rest (Commerce and Offices) Convention (No. 106) and Recommendation (No. 103), 1957.

4. *Paid leave*

Holidays with Pay Convention, 1936 (No. 52).

Holidays with Pay (Agriculture) Convention, 1952 (No. 101).

Holidays with Pay Convention (Revised), 1970 (No. 132).

Paid Educational Leave Convention (No. 140) and Recommendation (No. 148), 1974.

5. *Home work*

Home Work Convention (No. 177) and Recommendation (No. 184), 1996.

C. *Occupational safety and health*

1. *General provisions*

Prevention of Industrial Accidents Recommendation, 1929 (No. 31).

Protection of Workers' Health Recommendation, 1953 (No. 97).

Occupational Safety and Health Convention (No. 155) and Recommendation (No. 164), 1981.

Occupational Health Services Convention (No. 161) and Recommendation (No. 171), 1985.

Prevention of Major Industrial Accidents Convention (No. 174) and Recommendation (No. 181), 1993.

2. *Protection against specific risks*

Toxic substance and agents

Anthrax Prevention Recommendation, 1919 (No. 3).

Lead Poisoning (Women and Children) Recommendation, 1919 (No. 4).

White Lead (Painting) Convention, 1921 (No. 13).

Radiation Protection Convention (No. 115) and Recommendation (No. 114), 1960.

Benzene Convention (No. 136) and Recommendation (No. 144), 1971.

Occupational Cancer Convention (No. 139) and Recommendation (No. 147), 1974.

Asbestos Convention (No. 162) and Recommendation (No. 172), 1986.

Machinery

Guarding of Machinery Convention (No. 119) and Recommendation (No. 118), 1963.

Maximum weight

Maximum Weight Convention (No. 127) and Recommendation (No. 128), 1967.

Air pollution, noise and vibration

Working Environment (Air Pollution, Noise and Vibration) Convention (No. 148) and Recommendation (No. 156), 1977.

3. *Protection in given branches of activity*

Building industry

Safety Provisions (Building) Convention (No. 62) and Recommendation (No. 53), 1937.

Commerce and offices

Hygiene (Commerce and Offices) Convention (No. 120) and Recommendation (No. 120), 1964.

Construction

Safety and Health in Construction Convention (No. 167) and Recommendation (No. 175), 1988.

Dock work

Marking of Weight (Packages Transported by Vessels) Convention, 1929 (No. 27).

Protection against Accidents (Dockers) Convention, 1929 (No. 28).

Protection against Accidents (Dockers) Convention (Revised), 1932 (No. 32).

Occupational Safety and Health (Dock Work) Convention (No. 152) and Recommendation (No. 160), 1979.

Mines

Safety and Health in Mines Convention (No. 176) and Recommendation (No. 183), 1995.

D. *Social services, housing and leisure*

Welfare Facilities Recommendation, 1956 (No. 102).

Workers' Housing Recommendation, 1961 (No. 115).

Utilisation of Spare Time Recommendation, 1924 (No. 21).

VII. Social security

A. *Comprehensive standards*

(Covering the branches of social security enumerated in B below)

Social Security (Minimum Standards) Convention, 1952 (No. 102).

Income Security Recommendation, 1944 (No. 67).

Social Security (Armed Forces) Recommendation, 1944 (No. 68).

Equality of Treatment (Social Security) Convention, 1962 (No. 118).

Maintenance of Social Seçurity Rights Convention, 1982 (No. 157).

Maintenance of Social Security Rights Recommendation, 1983 (No. 167).

B. *Protection in the various social security branches*

1. *Medical care and sickness benefit*

Sickness Insurance (Industry) Convention, 1927 (No. 24).

Sickness Insurance (Agriculture) Convention, 1927 (No. 25).

Medical Care Recommendation, 1944 (No. 69).

Medical Care and Sickness Benefits Convention (No. 130) and Recommendation (No. 134), 1969.

2. *Old-age, invalidity and survivors' benefits*

Old-Age Insurance (Industry, etc.) Convention, 1933 (No. 35).

Old-Age Insurance (Agriculture) Convention, 1933 (No. 36).

Invalidity Insurance (Industry, etc.) Convention, 1933 (No. 37).

Invalidity Insurance (Agriculture) Convention, 1933 (No. 38).

Survivors' Insurance (Industry, etc.) Convention, 1933 (No. 39).

Survivors' Insurance (Agriculture) Convention, 1933 (No. 40).

Maintenance of Migrants' Pension Rights Convention, 1935 (No. 48).

Invalidity, Old-Age and Survivors' Benefits Convention (No. 128) and Recommendation (No. 131), 1967.

3. *Employment injury benefit*

Workmen's Compensation (Agriculture) Convention, 1921 (No. 12).

Workmen's Compensation (Accidents) Convention, 1925 (No. 17).

Workmen's Compensation (Occupational Diseases) Convention, 1925 (No. 18).

Equality of Treatment (Accident Compensation) Convention, 1925 (No. 19).

Workmen's Compensation (Occupational Diseases) Convention (Revised), 1934 (No. 42).

Employment Injury Benefits Convention, 1964 (No. 121) [Schedule I amended 1980].

Employment Injury Benefits Recommendation, 1964 (No. 121).

4. *Unemployment benefits*

Unemployment Provision Convention (No. 44) and Recommendation (No. 44), 1934.

5. *Maternity benefit*

Maternity Protection Convention, 1919 (No. 3).

Maternity Protection Convention (Revised) (No. 103) and Recommendation (No. 95), 1952.

6. *Family benefit*

See under A above.

VIII. Employment of women

See also I.C above: Equality of opportunity and treatment.

A. *Maternity protection*

Maternity Protection Convention, 1919 (No. 3).

Maternity Protection Convention (Revised) (No. 103) and Recommendation (No. 95), 1952.

B. *Night work*

Night Work (Women) Convention, 1919 (No. 4).

Night Work (Women) Convention (Revised), 1934 (No. 41).

Night Work (Women) Convention (Revised), 1948 (No. 89) [and Protocol, 1990].

C. *Underground work*

Underground Work (Women) Convention, 1935 (No. 45).

IX. Employment of children and young persons

A. *Minimum age*

Minimum Age (Industry) Convention, 1919 (No. 5).

Minimum Age (Industry) Convention (Revised), 1937 (No. 59).

Minimum Age (Non-Industrial Employment) Convention, 1932 (No. 33).

Minimum Age (Non-Industrial Employment) Convention (Revised), 1937 (No. 60).

Minimum Age (Agriculture) Convention, 1921 (No. 10).

Minimum Age (Underground Work) Convention (No. 123) and Recommendation (No. 124), 1965.

Minimum Age Convention (No. 138) and Recommendation (No. 146), 1973.

B. *Night work*

Night Work of Young Persons (Industry) Convention, 1919 (No. 6).

Night Work of Young Persons (Industry) Convention (Revised), 1948 (No. 90).

Night Work of Young Persons (Non-Industrial Occupations) Convention (No. 79) and Recommendation (No. 80), 1946.

C. *Medical examination*

Medical Examination of Young Persons (Industry) Convention, 1946 (No. 77).

Medical Examination of Young Persons (Non-Industrial Occupations) Convention, 1946 (No. 78).

Medical Examination of Young Persons Recommendation, 1946 (No. 79).

Medical Examination of Young Persons (Underground Work) Convention, 1965 (No. 124).

D. *Underground work*

Employment of Young Persons (Underground Work) Recommendation, 1965 (No. 125).

X. Older workers

Older Workers Recommendation, 1980 (No. 162).

XI. Migrant workers

Inspection of Emigrants Convention, 1926 (No. 21).

Migration for Employment Convention (Revised) (No. 97) and Recommendation (Revised) (No. 86), 1949.

Protection of Migrant Workers (Underdeveloped Countries) Recommendation, 1955 (No. 100).

Migrant Workers (Supplementary Provisions) Convention, 1975 (No. 143).

Migrant Workers Recommendation, 1975 (No. 151).

See also VII.A and B.2 above.

XII. Indigenous workers, tribal populations and workers in non-metropolitan territories

1. *Indigenous workers*

Recruiting of Indigenous Workers Convention, 1936 (No. 50).

Penal Sanctions (Indigenous Workers) Convention, 1939 (No. 65).

Abolition of Penal Sanctions (Indigenous Workers) Convention, 1955 (No. 104).

Contracts of Employment (Indigenous Workers) Convention, 1939 (No. 64).

Contracts of Employment (Indigenous Workers) Convention, 1947 (No. 86).

Elimination of Recruiting Recommendation, 1936 (No. 46).

2. *Workers in non-metropolitan territories*

Social Policy in Dependent Territories Recommendation, 1944 (No. 70).

Social Policy in Dependent Territories (Supplementary Provisions) Recommendation, 1945 (No. 74).

Social Policy (Non-Metropolitan Territories) Convention, 1947 (No. 82).

Right of Association (Non-Metropolitan Territories) Convention, 1947 (No. 84).

Labour Inspectorates (Non-Metropolitan Territories) Convention, 1947 (No. 85).

Labour Standards (Non-Metropolitan Territories) Convention, 1947 (No. 83).

3. *Indigenous and tribal populations*

Indigenous and Tribal Populations Convention (No. 107) and Recommendation (No. 104), 1957.

Indigenous and Tribal Populations Convention (Revised), 1989 (No. 169).

XIII. Other special categories

A. *Seafarers*

1. *General*

National Seamen's Codes Recommendation, 1920 (No. 9).

Seafarers' Identity Documents Convention, 1958 (No. 108).

Seafarers' Engagement (Foreign Vessels) Recommendation, 1958 (No. 107).

Employment of Seafarers (Technical Developments) Recommendation, 1970 (No. 139).

Continuity of Employment (Seafarers) Convention (No. 145) and Recommendation (No. 154), 1976.

Merchant Shipping (Minimum Standards) Convention, 1976 (No. 147) [and Protocol, 1996].

Merchant Shipping (Improvement of Standards) Recommendation, 1976 (No. 155).

2. *Training and entry into employment*

Placing of Seamen Convention, 1920 (No. 9).

Seamen's Articles of Agreement Convention, 1926 (No. 22).

Vocational Training (Seafarers) Recommendation, 1970 (No. 137).

Recruitment and Placement of Seafarers Convention (No. 179) and Recommendation (No. 186), 1996.

3. *Conditions for admission to employment*

Minimum Age (Sea) Convention, 1920 (No. 7).

Minimum Age (Trimmers and Stokers) Convention, 1921 (No. 15).

Minimum Age (Sea) Convention (Revised), 1936 (No. 58).

Minimum Age Convention (No. 138) and Recommendation (No. 146), 1973.

Medical Examination of Young Persons (Sea) Convention, 1921 (No. 16).

Medical Examination (Seafarers) Convention, 1946 (No. 73).

4. *Certificate of competency*

Officers' Competency Certificates Convention, 1936, (No. 53).

Certification of Ships' Cooks Convention, 1946 (No. 69).

Certification of Able Seamen Convention, 1946 (No. 74).

5. *General conditions of employment*

Wages, Hours of Work and Manning (Sea) Convention (Revised) (No. 109) and Recommendation (No. 109), 1958.

Repatriation of Seamen Convention, 1926 (No. 23).

Repatriation (Ship Masters and Apprentices) Recommendation, 1926 (No. 27).

Paid Vacations (Seafarers) Convention (Revised), 1949 (No. 91).

Seafarers' Annual Leave with Pay Convention, 1976 (No. 146).

Protection of Young Seafarers Recommendation, 1976 (No. 153).

Repatriation of Seafarers Convention (Revised) (No. 166) and Recommendation (No. 174), 1987.

Seafarers' Hours of Work and the Manning of Ships Convention (No. 180) and Seafarers' Wages, Hours of Work and the Manning of Ships Recommendation (No. 187), 1996.

6. *Safety, health and welfare*

Food and Catering (Ships' Crews) Convention, 1946 (No. 68).

Bedding, Mess Utensils and Miscellaneous Provisions (Ships' Crews) Recommendation, 1946 (No. 78).

Accommodation of Crews Convention (Revised), 1949 (No. 92).

Accommodation of Crews (Supplementary Provisions) Convention, 1970 (No. 133).

Crew Accommodation (Air Conditioning) Recommendation, 1970 (No. 140).

Crew Accommodation (Noise Control) Recommendation, 1970 (No. 141).

Ships' Medicine Chests Recommendation, 1958 (No. 105).

Medical Advice at Sea Recommendation, 1958 (No. 106).

Prevention of Accidents (Seafarers) Convention (No. 134) and Recommendation (No. 142), 1970.

Seamen's Welfare in Ports Recommendation, 1936 (No. 48).

Seafarers' Welfare Recommendation, 1970 (No. 138).

Seafarers' Welfare Convention (No. 163) and Recommendation (No. 173), 1987.

Health Protection and Medical Care (Seafarers) Convention (No. 164), 1987.

7. *Labour inspection*

Labour Inspection (Seamen) Recommendation, 1926 (No. 28).

Labour Inspection (Seafarers) Convention (No. 178) and Recommendation (No. 185), 1996.

8. *Social security*

Unemployment Indemnity (Shipwreck) Convention, 1920 (No. 8).

Unemployment Insurance (Seamen) Recommendation, 1920 (No. 10).

Shipowners' Liability (Sick and Injured Seamen) Convention, 1936 (No. 55).

Sickness Insurance (Sea) Convention, 1936 (No. 56).

Social Security (Seafarers) Convention, 1946 (No. 70).

Seafarers' Social Security (Agreements) Recommendation, 1946 (No. 75).

Seafarers' (Medical Care for Dependants) Recommendation, 1946 (No. 76).

Seafarers' Pensions Convention, 1946 (No. 71).

Social Security (Seafarers) Convention (Revised) (No. 165), 1987.

B. *Fishermen*

Hours of Work (Fishing) Recommendation, 1920 (No. 7).

Minimum Age (Fishermen) Convention, 1959 (No. 112).

Medical Examination (Fishermen) Convention, 1959 (No. 113).

Fishermen's Articles of Agreement Convention, 1959 (No. 114).

Fishermen's Competency Certificates Convention, 1966 (No. 125).

Accommodation of Crews (Fishermen) Convention, 1966 (No. 126).

Vocational Training (Fishermen) Recommendation, 1966 (No. 126).

C. *Inland navigation*

Hours of Work (Inland Navigation) Recommendation, 1920 (No. 8).

D. *Dockworkers*

Dock Work Convention (No. 137) and Recommendation (No. 145), 1973.

See also VI.C.3 above.

E. *Plantations*

Plantations Convention, 1958 (No. 110) [and Protocol, 1982].

Plantations Recommendation, 1958 (No. 110).

F. *Tenants and share-croppers*

Tenants and Share-Croppers Recommendation, 1968 (No. 132).

G. *Nursing personnel*

Nursing Personnel Convention (No. 149) and Recommendation (No. 157), 1977.

H. *Hotels and restaurants*

Working Conditions (Hotels and Restaurants) Convention (No. 172) and Recommendation (No. 179), 1991.

Appendix 2

Bibliography

Texts of international labour standards

International Labour Conventions and Recommendations, 1919-1995, Geneva, 1996 (3 vols.), with "Handbook of procedures relating to international labour Conventions and Recommendations" (pp. 425-466). (Separate leaflets are added for international labour standards adopted since 1996.)

The International Labour Code, 1951. A systematic arrangement of the Conventions and Recommendations adopted by the International Labour Conference, 1919-1951, with appendices embodying other standards of social policy framed by or with the co-operation of the International Labour Organisation, 1919-1951. Geneva, 1952 (2 vols.).

Summaries of international labour standards, second edition, Geneva, 1991.

Newly adopted Conventions and Recommendations are published in the *Official Bulletin* of the International Labour Office as well as in the form of separate leaflets. The *Official Bulletin* also publishes the texts of resolutions adopted by the International Labour Conference and by the Industrial Committees.

Codes of practice, model codes and guides

The following is a list of ILO codes of practice, model codes and guides in the field of occupational safety and health:

Accident prevention on board ship at sea and in port, Geneva, 1996, xiv + 194 pp.

Code of practice for the safe construction and installation of electric passenger, goods and service lifts, Geneva, 1972, 108 pp.

Guide to health and hygiene in agricultural work, Geneva, 1979, xiii + 309 pp.

Guide to safety and health in dock work, Geneva, 1988, x + 287 pp.

Guide to safety in agriculture, Geneva, 1969, xiii + 247 pp. and 68 illustrations.

Guide to the prevention and suppression of dust in mining, tunnelling and quarrying, Geneva, 1965, xvii + 421 pp.

Management of alcohol- and drug-related issues in the workplace, Geneva, 1996, xii + 61 pp.

Model code of safety regulations for underground work in coal mines for the guidance of governments and of the coal-mining industry, Geneva, 1950, 102 pp.

Occupational exposure to airborne substances harmful to health, Geneva, 1980, viii + 44 pp.

Occupational safety and health in the iron and steel industry, Geneva, 1983, x + 343 pp.

Prevention of accidents due to electricity underground in coal mines, Geneva, 1959, 54 pp.

Prevention of accidents due to explosions underground in coal mines, Geneva, 1974, 37 pp.

Prevention of accidents due to fires underground in coal mines, Geneva, 1959, 48 pp.

Prevention of major industrial accidents, Geneva, 1991, xiii + 108 pp.

Protection of workers against noise and vibration in the working environment, Geneva, 1977, vii + 74 pp. (out of print).

Protection of workers' personal data, Geneva, 1997, ix + 47 pp.

Radiation protection of workers (ionising radiations), Geneva, 1987.

Recording and notification of occupational accidents and diseases, Geneva, 1996, xxi + 97 pp.

Safe construction and installation of escalators, Recommendations adopted by the International Committee for Lift Regulations (CIRA) on 6 June 1972, Geneva, 1976, iii + 29 pp. (Occupational Safety and Health Series, No. 28).

Safe construction and operation of tractors, Geneva, 1976, ix + 39 pp.

Safe design and use of chain saws, Geneva, 1978, x + 72 pp.

Safety and health in agricultural work, Geneva, 1965, viii + 132 pp. (out of print).

Safety and health in building and civil engineering work, Geneva, 1972, xii + 386 pp.

Safety and health in dock work, revised edition, Geneva, 1977, xvi + 221 pp.

Safety and health in coal mines, Geneva, 1986, xiv + 176 pp.

Safety and health in forestry work, Geneva, 1998, xii + 200 pp. (estimated).

Safety and health in opencast mines, Geneva, 1991, xiii + 121 pp.

Safety and health in shipbuilding and ship repairing, Geneva, 1974, viii + 260 pp.

Safety and health in the construction of fixed offshore installations in the petroleum industry, Geneva, 1982, xi + 135 pp.

Safety and health in the use of agrochemicals: A guide, Geneva, 1991, x + 79 pp.

Safety and health in the use of chemicals at work, Geneva, 1993, xi + 95 pp.

Safety and health in the use of chemicals at work: A training manual, Abu Bakar Che Man and David Gold, Geneva, 1993, ix + 78 pp.

Safety, health and working conditions in the transfer of technology to developing countries, Geneva, 1988, xi + 81 pp.

Safety in the use of asbestos, Geneva, 1984, xlii + 116 pp.

Your health and safety at work: A modular training package, Geneva, 1996, 11 modules + 2 appendices.

In addition to these codes of practice, guides and modules, the *ILO Encyclopaedia of Occupational Health and Safety* (fourth edition), Geneva, 1998, is an essential reference (available as a four-volume set and a CD-ROM) for standards in this field; and the Occupational Safety and Health Series (ISSN 0078-3129) includes around 70 titles on specific health and safety topics.

Other publications

Alcock, A. *History of the International Labour Organisation*, London, Macmillan, and New York, Octagon Books, 1971.

Ghebali, V.-Y. *L'Organisation internationale du Travail*, Geneva, Georg, 1987.

Haas, E.B. *Human rights and international action: The case of freedom of association*, Stanford, California, Stanford University Press, 1970.

ILO. *The International Labour Organization – The first decade*, London, Allen and Unwin, 1931.

— *The ILO and human rights*, Report of the Director-General (Part 1) to the International Labour Conference, 52nd Session, 1968, report presented by the International Labour Organisation to the International Conference on Human Rights, 1968, Geneva, 1968.

— *Freedom by dialogue: Economic development by social progress – The ILO contributions*, Report of the Director-General, Part 1, International Labour Conference, 56th Session, Geneva, 1971.

— *Freedom of association: Digest of decisions of the Freedom of Association Committee of the Governing Body of the ILO*, second edition, Geneva, 1976.

— *Social policy in a changing world: The ILO response*, Selected speeches by Wilfred Jenks, Director-General of the International Labour Office, 1970-1973, Geneva, 1976.

— *The impact of international labour Conventions and Recommendations*, Geneva, 1976.

— Report of the Working Party on International Labour Standards, *Official Bulletin*, Vol. LXX, 1987, Series A.

— *Human rights – A common responsibility*, Report of the Director-General (Part 1) to the International Labour Conference, 75th Session, Geneva, 1988.

— *Trade unions and the ILO*, second (revised) edition, A workers' education manual, Geneva, 1988.

— *Trade union participation in shaping and adopting international labour standards*, course topic, Geneva, 1986 (Workers' Education Branch).

— *Trade union participation in implementing international labour standards*, course topic, Geneva, 1986 (Workers' Education Branch).

— *Trade union participation in the ILO supervisory system for the protection of trade union rights*, course topic, Geneva, 1989 (Workers' Education Branch).

— *The ILO in the service of social progress. A workers' education manual*, second edition, Geneva, 1995.

— *ILO law on freedom of association: Standards and procedures*, Geneva, 1995.

— *Freedom of association. Digest of decisions and principles of the Freedom of Association Committee of the Governing Body*, fourth edition, Geneva, 1996.

— *Maritime labour Conventions and Recommendations*, fourth edition, Geneva, 1998.

Jenks, C. W. *The international protection of trade union freedom*, London, Stevens and Sons, 1957.

— *Human rights and international labour standards*, London, Stevens and Sons; New York, F.A. Praeger, 1960.

— *Social justice in the law of nations: The ILO impact after fifty years*, London, Oxford University Press, 1970.

(See also under ILO: *Social policy in a changing world*.)

Johnston, G.A. *The International Labour Organisation: Its work for social and economic progress*, London, Europa Publications, 1970.

Landy, E.A. *The effectiveness of international supervision: Thirty years of ILO experience*, London, Stevens and Sons; Dobb's Ferry, New York, Oceana Publications. 1966.

Plant, R. *Labour standards and structural adjustment*, Geneva, ILO, 1994.

Phelan, E. J. *Yes and Albert Thomas*. New York, Columbia University Press, 1949.

Scelle, G. *L'Organisation internationale du Travail et le BIT*, Paris, M. Rivière, 1930.

Servais, J.M. *International Labour Organisation*. The Hague, Kluwer Law International, 1996.

Shotwell, J. T. *The origins of the International Labor Organization*, New York, Columbia University Press, 1934, 2 vols.

Troclet, L.-E. *Législation sociale internationale*, Brussels, Editions de la Librairie Encyclopédique, 1952, 3 vols.

Valticos, N. *International labour law*, second edition, Deventer, Kluwer, 1995.

Application of international labour standards in particular member States (from the International Labour Review*)*

Abdeljaouad, A. "The influence of international labour Conventions on Tunisian legislation", in *International Labour Review*, Mar. 1965, pp. 191-209.

Albalate Lafita, J. "The influence of international labour Conventions on labour law and social change in Spain", in *International Labour Review*, July-Aug. 1979, pp. 443-457.

Ayissi Mvodo, V. and Le Faou, R. "Influence of international labour standards on the legislation of Cameroon", in *International Labour Review*, Aug.-Sep. 1973, pp. 163-185.

Badaoui, A. Z. "The influence of international labour Conventions on the Arab Labour Standards Convention", in *International Labour Review*, Nov. 1970, pp. 475 -496.

Berenstein, A. "The influence of international labour Conventions on Swiss legislation", in *International Labour Review*, June 1958, pp. 495-518.

Cashell, M. "Influence on Irish law and practice of international labour standards", in *International Labour Review*, July 1972, pp. 47-73.

Charnovitz, S. "The influence of international labour standards on the world trading regime: A historical overview", in *International Labour Review*, Sep.-Oct. 1987, pp. 565-584.

Dahl, K.N. "The influence of ILO standards on Norwegian legislation", in *International Labour Review*, Sep. 1964, pp. 226-251.

"The European Social Charter and international labour standards", in *International Labour Review*, Nov. 1961, pp. 354-375, and Dec. 1961, pp. 462-477.

Hanami, T. "The influence of ILO standards on law and practice in Japan", in *International Labour Review*, Nov.-Dec. 1981, pp. 765-779.

"The influence of international labour Conventions on Nigerian labour legislation", in *International Labour Review*, July 1960, pp. 26-43.

"International labour standards and Asian countries", in *International Labour Review*, Apr. 1961, pp. 303-321.

Ivanov, S. A. "International labour Conventions and the USSR", in *International Labour Review*, Apr. 1966, pp. 401-413.

Johnston, G. A. "The influence of international labour standards on legislation and practice in the United Kingdom", in *International Labour Review*, May 1968, pp. 465- 487.

Kalula, E. "The influence of international labour standards on Zambian legislation", in *International Labour Review*, Sep.-Oct. 1985, pp. 593-610.

Lagergren, S. "The influence of ILO standards on Swedish law and practice", in *International Labour Review*, May-June 1986, pp. 305-328.

Landau, C. E. "The influence of ILO standards on Australian labour law and practice", in *International Labour Review*, Nov.-Dec. 1987, pp. 669-690.

Menon, V. K. R. "The influence of international labour Conventions on Indian labour legislation", in *International Labour Review*, June 1956, pp. 551-571.

Morellet, J. "The influence of international labour Conventions on French legislation", in *International Labour Review*, Apr. 1970, pp. 331-358.

Mrachkov, V. "International labour Conventions and Bulgarian legislation", in *International Labour Review*, Mar.-Apr. 1979, pp. 205-221.

Pesic, R. "International labour standards and Yugoslav legislation", in *International Labour Review*, Nov. 1967, pp. 443-467.

Plata-Castilla, A. "International labour standards and Colombian legislation", in *International Labour Review*, Feb. 1969, pp. 137-158.

Riva-Sanseverino, L. "The influence of international labour Conventions on Italian labour legislation", in *International Labour Review*, June 1961, pp. 576-601.

Rosner, J. "Influence of international labour Conventions on Polish legislation", in *International Labour Review*, Nov. 1965, pp. 353-379.

Samson, K. "Changing pattern of ILO supervision", in *International Labour Review*, Sep.-Oct. 1979, pp. 569-587.

Schnorr, G. "The influence of ILO standards on law and practice in the Federal Republic of Germany", in *International Labour Review*, Dec. 1974, pp. 539-564.

Servais, J.M. "Flexibility and rigidity in international labour standards", in *International Labour Review*, Mar.-Apr. 1986, pp. 193-208.

Süssekind, A. "The influence of international labour standards on Brazilian legislation", in *International Labour Review*, July-Aug. 1984, pp. 441-456.

Troclet, L.-E., and Vogel-Polsky, E. "The influence of international labour Conventions on Belgian labour legislation", in *International Labour Review*, Nov. 1968, pp. 389-424.

Valticos, N. "The influence of international labour Conventions on Greek legislation", in *International Labour Review*, June 1955, pp. 593-615.

— "Future prospects for international labour standards", in *International Labour Review*, Nov.-Dec. 1979, pp. 679-697.